GOOD CATS

GOOD CATS

The Complete Guide to Cat Training

•

Elizabeth Kaplan
and
Michael A. Kaplan

ILLUSTRATED BY 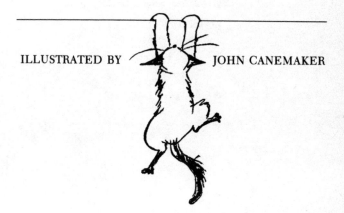 JOHN CANEMAKER

A PERIGEE BOOK

Perigee Books
are published by
The Putnam Publishing Group
200 Madison Avenue
New York, NY 10016

The authors gratefully acknowledge Little, Brown and Company for permission
to quote from "The Kitten," which appears in *Verses from 1929 On* by Ogden
Nash. Copyright 1940 by the Curtis Publishing Company.

Library of Congress Cataloging in Publication Data

Kaplan, Elizabeth, date.
Good cats.

1. Cats—Training.   I. Kaplan, Michael A.
II. Title.
SF446.6.K37   1985   636.808′8   85-595
ISBN 0-399-51117-2 (pbk.)

Printed in the United States of America
1   2   3   4   5   6   7   8   9   10

To Calico . . .

our first.

Contents

Introduction
Keeping the Kitten in Your Cat

The trouble with a kitten is
That
Eventually it becomes a
Cat.

—OGDEN NASH

It is hard to find anyone who doesn't like kittens—and admits it! How could they?

Kittens are small bundles of spunk and fluff, universal delights. They have an inborn sense of discovery and adventure and are continually turning new corners, getting into everything, and letting the world know their pride of accomplishment at devastating a frightening adversary—even when that opponent is nothing more than an overstuffed chair.

Kittens are paradoxes of wiry strength and agility packaged as warm balls of fur that purr at the slightest touch. Their eyes are wide open for any signal from their owners to play and to learn. Kittens are, by their very nature, adorable creatures.

But in a few months, a kitten will turn into a cat, and confessed cat haters are all too easy to find. They particularly dislike a lazy feline, one whose primary function in life is to whine about his dinner and take up space. These "catophobes" envision a distasteful combination of yowling, scratching, and indifference; a pet who is more of a burden than a joy.

Unfortunately, there are cats whose behavior justifies such low esteem. And in almost every case, it is the owner who is responsible. As the kitten loses the natural physical appeal of babyhood, many owners lose interest. An ignored cat has no choice but to settle into a lonely life of boredom. And his interest in humans is one of the first things to go. But if you take an active interest in your pet, this household tragedy need not occur. After all, creating a healthy relationship between you and your cat is the key to enjoying your new pet and to training him to be an obedient cat.

This book is a training manual. We'll tell you how to keep the lively sense of fun and intrigue from being conditioned out of your cat, and how to minimize or eliminate the many bad habits cats can grow into. Meanwhile, you'll be gaining your cat's trust and friendship in the process. It takes some time on your part, and a lot of patience, but the rewards will be reaped for as long as you own your cat.

Your cat is able and willing to cooperate on this journey for the entire route. You must be able and willing to open the necessary doors and post the appropriate signs along the way. Take your time as you proceed and enjoy all your sessions with your cat. The more fun you have, the more fun your cat will have.

After years of cat training, we have devised a program that appeals to cats. In our system, *you* create the proper environment in which to allow your cat to learn. Your cat, however, is convinced he is *teaching himself*. A common mistake cat owners make is to use dog-training techniques on their cat. When this approach fails—and it is doomed to fail—resentment fills the air and neither cat nor owner is happy with the outcome.

One of the goals in dog training is to achieve stern dominance over the pooch. Master is usually found ordering his dog to do this or that: "Come," "Stay," "Heel," "Fetch." When a dog refuses to respond properly, he is reprimanded in no uncertain terms that he is a "bad dog." This approach is effective because of the dog's guilty conscience, a characteristic *unknown* to cats.

Such an approach is meaningless to cats because of their inbred sense of independence combined with all cats' presumption of equality with their owners. Cats are more apt to respond favorably to a request than to a demand. So remember not to expect the slavish obedience of a common dog; we are dealing with a proud and intelligent creature. Neither kittens nor cats have a desire to perform tricks, and we are not going to attempt such debasing activities.

Many of the "bad" things a cat is likely to do are performed in the spirit of harmless fun more than anything else, and cannot be considered as seriously destructive behavior. Keeping this devilishly playful side of a kitten's personality, without the unpleasant side effects, is an important part of the program outlined in this book.

As for those "bad" things a cat does that really are bad, we can help there too. Together we can *change* your cat's behavior.

Does your cat ignore you when you call out his name? We can tell you how to get him to come to you and to do it consistently in two weeks or less.

Is your cat changing the pattern of your upholstery with his claws? We can show you how to curb this destructive habit.

Is your cat fat and terminally lazy? We will lead you through a program that can get your cat back in shape.

Are you spending a fortune at the local pet store on toys your cat won't even look at? We will show you how to get your cat active and interested in "toys" you may already have at home.

Are you unable to allow your cat to savor life in the outside world because you live in a city or too near a heavily trafficked road? Our leash training can make your cat eager to go on controlled, supervised walks with you.

Does the thought of a single cat left alone in a small apartment while you spend the day at work leave you feeling guilty? We can help you get over the worries of the "latch-key" cat.

Can't keep kitty off tables, shelves, or other designated off-limits areas? Problems in maintaining good toilet habits? Do you want to bring a new pet into your household, but are afraid kitty won't allow it? These challenges and many more can be handled by applying the simple techniques laid out for you in the following chapters.

All animal-training courses are most effective if begun during the impressionable first few months of the animal's life, but even fully grown cats can benefit from the approach found in these pages. Our program can help cats of all ages and types—from purebreds to alley cats—become happier cats and positive additions to your home.

Many cat lovers *like* a quiet, lazy animal who sleeps his life away. And nature has given cats the need for almost sixteen hours of sleep daily. Really! But even those who desire a lap cat who is all lap will find many benefits in our program.

Cats are naturally dependable and self-reliant. Through our course, nothing of your cat's inbred grooming nature, sanitary habits, or maternal instincts (should your cat be a she) is lost. We will tell you how to retain as much of a kitten's personality as possible, while losing none of a cat's maturity or native intelligence. How can you lose? And with a little bit of luck—and a lot of love—you will keep the kitten in your cat.

1
Bringing Home Baby

There's no doubt about it; a new kitten will bring delight into any home for years to come. But as easy as it seems to raise a kitten, you must start right from the beginning to ensure a long and happy relationship with your new cat.

First and foremost, you must be ready to take on this new daily responsibility. In the beginning, your new cat will require extra time and attention from you every day, so you must pick the right moment for adopting your kitten (a month before you leave for vacation is not a good time).

If the time is right and you are going to adopt that adorable cat who stepped right up and nuzzled your ear, well, who can blame you! Here is a basic checklist of items you should have ready *before* bringing kitty home that will help him feel comfortable and secure and will give you the best advantage for successful training.

Kitty's Own Bed. This can be a basket, or a box with sides that kitty can climb over, lined with an old blanket, quilt, pillow, or anything that will provide kitty with the two things he most craves: a soft and warm place to curl up and the protected feeling of a "nest." You can improvise with a laundry basket, a drawer, or whatever you have on hand. Just make sure kitty has easy access to it.

A Feeding Bowl and a Water Bowl. You will need two bowls, one for water and one for food. Any small bowls will do; heavier ones stay in place better. If you want to spend the money, get weighted pet bowls so kitty doesn't have trouble keeping them in one spot!

Food. There are three basic types: dry kitten food for his basic diet (you should moisten it with warm water for the first month); canned cat food for variety (only about one-quarter of a can, three times a week at first); and special "treat" food, either a commercial product or perhaps some chicken liver or fish. (In the beginning, give treats in infinitesimal quantities, really just enough for kitty to lick off your finger. You are using them to establish trust, not to nourish kitty. They should be a signal to him that life with you may not be all that bad even if it looks awfully chaotic!) Never overuse treats, especially with a kitten, whose digestive system isn't ready for such rich foods. Naturally, though, his palate is quite ready to be spoiled!

A Cat Carrier. You can buy one at a pet store, particularly if you anticipate traveling with your cat, or you can use a secure box with holes in it (make sure they're not too big, as kittens look bigger than they really are and can squeeze out of anything they can get their head through!). A large towel wrapped snugly around the kitten's body and paws is also fine if you've brought along someone else to do the driving. Don't, however, attempt a collar and leash at this point, for kitty is both too small and too weak to handle one.

A Litter Box. Start with a low-rimmed model so kitty can

get in and out easily. This box, filled with fresh kitty litter, should be set up in its proper place from day one. Cats use their litter almost by instinct and they learn where it is immediately, so don't keep changing the box's location.

A *Pooper Scooper*. Start clean, stay clean! Get yourself right into the habit of keeping kitty's litter clean—every day. (A slotted kitchen spoon will do the trick.)

A *Scratching Pad*. The best and cheapest scratching pad is one you build yourself (see Chapter 6). A kitten who learns to scratch it right away will probably never need to be trained not to use the couch—because he will have a *choice,* and he will choose *his* spot, the one that allows him to do his necessary scratching without being interrupted by you!

Before you bring your new kitten home, do a little "kitty-proofing" around your house. Kitty-proofing? Sure, just as you would for a small child. Make sure all cabinets containing harmful cleaning or medical supplies are securely fastened. And don't forget that kittens can jump.

Check loose electrical cords and even nonelectrical cords (like those for your drapes) to be sure they are well out of kitty's reach. If these can't be removed or placed safely out of reach, it is a good idea to tape them down until kitty is old enough to be trained to stay away from them.

Until you are ready to begin outdoor training with your cat, make sure all regularly opened doors and windows are securely screened. (Now is a good time to repair that hole in the screen you've meaning to get to!) If you have a basement full of junk or old paint cans and wish it to be off limits to kitty, make sure he has no access to it.

Remember just how small a two- to three-month-old kitten is; he can get just about anywhere he pleases. If you don't want him behind your refrigerator, couch, or antique breakfront, you must block off these areas *before* you bring kitty home or that undoubtedly will be the first place he heads for.

In the beginning, keep your toilet seat cover down, don't leave any tub of water unattended, and make sure someone is watching if the stove is in use.

In general, bear in mind that your kitten has not yet learned what household dangers *are*, let alone how to avoid them. So you must look out *for* him, just as you would for a small child. When you do have occasion to leave your cat alone, make sure there is nothing harmful he can get into. Kittens are never too young to be curious!

The Big Day

Choose a date when you can be home for the entire day and the house will be relatively quiet. It is best not to have too many people coming and going so that kitty has several uninterrupted, quiet hours to relax and explore his new home.

On his trip home, kitty should be kept warm and comfortable. Do not, under any circumstances, let him roam freely in the car. He will be nervous and will try to find a good hiding place—probably right under the gas pedal!

If possible, see that kitty has nothing to eat for a few hours before you leave. This will serve two purposes. First, a nervous kitten may have a hard time taking a car ride on a full stomach, and second, he will be sure to be hungry upon arriving at his new home. His very first impression of his new house can be finding something yummy to eat. Maybe this place won't be so bad after all!

Once you get your kitten home, let him go where he pleases and begin to explore his new surroundings. Don't fret if he runs behind the stove or a heavy cabinet and stays there for an hour or so. He will come out all by himself— and if he can't, he'll loudly let you know! Your cat will feel more secure knowing this safe retreat exists.

Within the first half hour or so at home, introduce kitty to his litter box. Make sure he sees where you are taking him so he can learn his own way. (After his initial use of it, he will be able to locate the box by his strong sense of smell.) Then simply put him in the box, take one of his paws, and gently demonstrate a digging motion. His instincts will quickly make the rest of the connection. Keep a close eye on his litter behavior for the first three days or so and carry him to the litter box regularly until you notice he is taking the initiative all on his own. And, of course, praise him incessantly for every little triumph.

Your cat will begin to relax after a few hours in your home. He won't hide, and his eyes will appear alert and curious. This is a good time to show him his feeding area. Have a small amount of food laid out and a couple of spoonfuls of milk in a separate bowl. Fill another bowl with fresh water. Remember to use low-rimmed bowls so kitty can reach the food and drink easily. The milk is a special welcoming treat; it should not become a regular part of your cat's diet, but in the beginning it will be something familiar to him and will help him relax and get used to his new home.

Don't be surprised if he doesn't dig right in. Your cat will still be a little nervous and even a bit confused. Tap your finger *in* the bit of milk to keep kitty's attention and hold a drop of it on your finger in front of his nose. He'll sniff and then lick. He'll catch on before long. Do not bring the food into any room your cat happens to be in. Begin right now to keep the food where *you* want the feeding area to be. With the litter box in one part of your house, food in another, and a play area in yet another, kitty will be encouraged to explore the house and will quickly learn not to be frightened of what's out there.

After a few hours of running around, eating, and discovering his new territory, your kitten will be tired out. Now's the perfect time to show him his bed. It's a good idea to put the bed in a spot that has a sense of natural shelter to help him feel comfortable and protected. If kitty isn't taking to the spot you have chosen for him, watch him those first few days. Where does he tend to spend the most time? On a shelf in your linen closet? Under your coffee table? He's giving you signals. Most cats head for warmth (a sunny windowsill or a heating vent) and shelter (under a table, behind the desk, or in between two pieces of furniture). Your cat will let you know what suits him the best. Once you've located the right spot, pick him up and take him there frequently so he can learn that it's his very own place. Don't be alarmed if kitty seems to be sleeping an awful lot during those first few weeks—remember, he's just a baby!

Of course, *your* bed is a pretty swell spot too, *if* you want it to be. For every owner who wishes his cat to spend the night curled up next to him in bed, there is another who wants to keep kitty out of the bedroom. If you fall into the latter category, you should establish this rule from the very first night. Your kitten may stand and cry just outside your door, but unless he has a real reason to feel frightened— like an overly friendly family dog—don't break down. You may have to show this kitten his bed several times in the beginning, but don't give in even just for one night because he will remember that he *can* get his own way.

If kitty seems lonely the first few nights, try wrapping a windup ticking clock (no electric cords or batteries, please) in a towel or light blanket and place it next to him in his bed. Spend a few minutes with him until he starts to get sleepy; he'll probably purr away. Then leave him with his "companion" and go to bed yourself. Your kitten will quickly learn this nighttime routine—and will adjust to *your* lifestyle, not the other way around.

Now that your cat is comfortable in his new home, it's time to start a bit of training. Even during these early moments with your cat it is never too early to gently reprimand him or move him away from areas you wish to maintain as off limits. But keep in mind that for a cat, at this early age especially, human contact is of utmost importance. It is also one of the keys to making your cat a *people* cat. A cat who wants to be part of the household and all that is going on around him. A cat who will become interested in changes. A cat who loves to greet visitors and relatives. A cat who is used to being picked up will be easier to train, easier to take out of the house, better behaved at the vet's or under a stranger's care. The more you pick up your cat, the more he will come to trust you and the easier it will be to establish a real bond between the two of you.

But don't force your cat to stay in your arms when he has had enough. Too much forced contact can mean raising a cat who hates to be held and who may even grow to resent you. In the beginning, hold your cat for just a few moments. As he becomes accustomed to it, his body will relax (you'll feel the difference in his muscles) and he will begin to purr. Then you may hold him for as long as you like. Soon he will feel free to sit on your lap, and a lifetime relationship will be established.

*   *   *

Everyone loves to play with a new kitten. If anything, you will have to caution your children to share kitty's attention *gently*. No tugging or pulling kitty! Remember how large the smallest human looks to a kitten who fits in the palm of your hand.

Playing *is* a good way to get your cat to relax and enjoy those first scary hours in his new home. All kittens love to play, and very few will resist a moving mouse on a string. They'll become so involved in the game that they'll forget there was ever anything to be afraid of. And if you get down on the floor during these early times together, your physical presence will be much less imposing. You'll simply become that swell, though big, person who gives kitty toys and food and shelter and warmth and hugs and friends and hiding places and even a clean bathroom.

Of course, pet your new cat and scratch him frequently. It's time to get to know him as an individual so you can find the perfect name for him. Once you have, use it and use it and use it again—it's never too early to christen kitty!

2
Christening Kitty

Cats are notoriously bossy. It's in their nature. You shouldn't fight it, but you can deal with it. A domestic cat is not as independent as he imagines himself to be. By allowing your cat the *illusion* of free choice, you will win half the battle for proper control on the sly.

Doing this requires establishing a healthy relationship between you and your cat. Remember, your cat must learn certain domestic routines from you, his owner. He may be a "domestic" cat, but you must help him fit into your domicile. The first step is crucial. You must correctly choose your cat's name.

Pity the kitten without a name of his own, or who has had changing owners and changing names. This cat comes to the plate with two strikes already against him. A cat's name is the key to the entire program you choose for him. A cat who responds to his name is ready to play or cuddle, but without a name your cat has *no choice at all*.

Cats generally do pretty much what they want to do.

Teaching your cat his name will allow you to offer many alternative activities to your cat that he will want to follow up on. Curiosity won't kill your cat—it will go a long way toward keeping the kitten in your cat.

Choosing a name is harder than you might think. You have to like it, your cat has to like it, and, most importantly, it has to work. Watch your kitten for a few days. Does he remind you of a friend or relative? Does he look like an Egyptian god or goddess, or a famous movie star? If nothing comes to mind, thumb through a favorite book and search out a name you like.

Once you think you have found an appropriate name, test it out. Try calling it out loud. Listen to yourself as you do this. Does it sound too much like a common phrase you use often? If so, the name may confuse your cat and you should look for something more distinctive. Eventually, your cat will not only respond to your unique tone of voice, but will actually know his name and will respond when other people call him.

If the name you're testing has three or more syllables, make sure a shorter nickname can be derived from it. Maxwell Q. Poindexter may fit your cat's personality, but it's quite a jumble of sounds for him to associate with himself and consistently respond to. Dexter or Max, however, would do very well with all those percussive sounds.

If you inherit a pre-named cat (and he knows his name), it is best for your cat and his future training to stick with it. But if you absolutely can't live with it, try this method. Reduce the existing name to its shortest form and then combine it with the new name you've chosen. For example, if you get a cat who answers to Barbara but you want to name her Katherine, call her "Kate-Barb." (Always put the *new* name in front, or else the cat will hear only the original name.) This cat will respond to the "Barb" half right away and will soon get used to "Kate-Barb." In a month of so, you'll be able to drop the "Barb."

If you adopt a full-grown cat and don't know what his name was, treat this cat like a kitten for name-training purposes. But don't be surprised if the name training takes a little longer.

Now that you have found the perfect name, one that you enjoy saying—and will really use—you must teach it to your cat. Begin by using the name constantly in any situation that would naturally pique your cat's curiosity. Feeding time is particularly appropriate, but be sure you find other occasions and situations for name training too, or Dexter might wind up thinking his name is synonymous with food. For example, make it a habit to introduce your cat to anyone entering the room; start training sessions by using the name to attract your cat's attention; and *always* use the cat's name when handling him.

Remember to repeat the name several times during these encounters. In the beginning, you may need to clap your hands just before calling out your cat's name. Only clap one time. Your cat usually won't need an ovation to attract his attention. During and after play continue to use the name. Toss a stringed toy or a small ball to your cat for about five minutes, then stop. When your cat starts to wander off, reclaim his attention by saying his name and resuming the game. Your cat will begin to associate your calling his name with many different pleasurable activities and will know to expect your full attention at those times. Dexter will soon feel it's worth checking out whatever might be going on when his name is called—even a quick scratch behind the ears or a comfortable lap rewards the effort of a trip!

If you have an outdoor cat, you may wish to incorporate a whistle with your regular name calling. Use an easily recognizable pattern and, as with a name, stick with the same one. This too should be repeated frequently at first.

During the first month you have your cat or kitten, you must call out his name and offer him a bit of attention *continually*. Within two weeks, you should start to notice a good response from your cat. Follow up with affectionate approval. Some cats take a bit longer to learn their name, but with *you* leading the way, they *will* learn it.

When your cat knows his name, you will have a handle on his overall behavior.

3
Just Who's in Charge Here?

Cats *can* be man's best friend. They offer love and companionship in large measures, yet they require little care and make fewer demands on their owners than any other domesticated animal. Independent and self-sufficient in thinking, a cat's main drawback stems from uncontrolled curiosity. But by following our three-point plan of behavior discipline, you can have the necessary control over this curiosity and can help your cat become the perfect pet.

Here is the agenda:

1. Train your cat to come when called.
2. Train your cat to allow you to pick him up comfortably and hold him when *you* find it necessary.
3. Train *yourself* to know when and how to use effective techniques that will instantly deter any bad behavior from your cat.

In the previous chapter, we discussed the importance of giving your cat a satisfactory name and teaching that name to him. Now we can move ahead to real training: teaching your cat to come when you call his name. Many cat owners think this is impossible to do, but cats *do* respond. Is there a cat alive who does not know the sound of a can opener in use and won't dash over immediately to discover what's been opened? Or who doesn't come at the sound of a refrigerator door opening? Even a kitten comes running at the sound of a fork tapping on his feeding bowl. This is a pet smart enough to connect specific sounds with specific activities, but it's up to you to use this inherent intelligence for training purposes.

Nine times out of ten, you will be opening the refrigerator or the can for yourself, but no matter how often your cat is disappointed by his curiosity, he will continue to show up in expectation—looking, no doubt, like the cat who expects to swallow the canary. Obviously, feeding time is a splendid opportunity to begin training your cat to come at the sound of his name. It won't be long before he associates his name with the pleasure of eating. "Stimuli" is the operative word here. Give your cat enough of a reason to come, and he will show up. And surely you can make yourself as interesting as a can of cat food.

While tapping a dish is effective for many cat owners, it is too closely tied to the feeding routine to be an effective calling device in the long run. In the beginning, you might wish to bribe your cat with food treats occasionally. But don't overdo food as an incentive; the purpose is to make the cat answer your call because he likes you, trusts you, and finds *you* interesting.

Start by getting your cat's attention. At this point in training, your cat already knows his name. Use it to your advantage: call him. You will probably receive just a look in response. That's fine. You *have* caught his attention.

Now, before you lose it, say "Come!" and repeat his

name. At the same time, gently tap the cushion next to where you are seated. The motion of your hand will sustain your cat's interest. Repeat the "Come" command and your cat's name a few times. If your cat simply stares at you like you're the village idiot, don't despair. Get up and walk calmly to your cat. Pick him up and slowly take him to the spot you indicated before with the hand-tapping motion. Repeat the "Come" command and your cat's name. Seat yourself next to your cat, tell him what a good cat he is, how pleased you are with him, and stroke him behind the ears, under the chin, or wherever he likes it best.

That's it! Nothing else for now. Cats are smart. Your cat will remember this session. You have just given him a nice experience, and this experience is associated with his name and the word "Come." Not a bad start for training.

So, you ask, why shouldn't I do it right over again? Please remember, we are *teaching* a cat, not training a dog. Dogs need to be devoted to someone, and they demonstrate this through slavish obedience. Cats respond, as the old saying goes, through curiosity. Once a cat has seen what you have to offer and his curiosity has been satisfied, he has no need to check it out again. So wait until the next time you happen to settle down in a different chair to begin another calling session.

It might work to your advantage to hold a toy or a piece of yarn at this stage in training. But, like food treats, this device should not be overused.

It is sometimes effective to call your cat when you are not in the same room with him so he cannot see whether responding to your call will be worth the trip. (That piece of yarn—or your undivided attention—*will* make it worth the trip.) It is often true that the farther you are from your cat, the more likely he is to respond to your call.

*   *   *

Once your cat is comfortable responding to you on a first-name basis, the next step is getting him to accept being held when *you* feel it is necessary. This is extremely important as a basic method of stopping bad behavior, since it obviously allows you to pluck your cat away from areas you wish to keep cat-free. But it can become an absolute necessity if your cat is ever in a truly dangerous situation.

Creatures as independent as cats often resist being picked up and held, but if you begin picking up your cat from the first day he enters your house, he will become accustomed to it and will trust your touch. Without this sense of trust, your cat may scratch you and dash off into unknown troubles or danger.

A properly held cat will feel comfortable and secure in your arms, never frightened or panicky. A mother cat may pick up a kitten by the scruff of his neck, but don't you try it! Hold your cat by supporting his back feet and bottom with your right hand while the curve of your arm cradles his back. Use your left hand to support his head, neck, and front paws. Your cat is in a basically upright, sitting position, facing left. (This description is for right-handed owners. Lefties should reverse the instructions.) Use this configuration as a guideline, not a firm and unwavering rule. The main idea is to keep a firm yet comfortable hold that truly supports your cat and lets him feel safe and secure.

To make your cat trust you implicitly, you must pick him up on a daily basis for his entire life. Just remember not to intrude on his dinner or play time. Don't catch your cat off guard and startle him, either. Your aim is control based on trust, so that you are in charge without any conflict.

In highly charged situations, you can gain added control by holding the scruff of your cat's neck firmly. This is acceptable as a control mechanism if, and only if, the main weight of your cat is being taken care of by your other hand. Holding your cat in this manner is effective but should only be used in an emergency. Once the "crisis" is over, give your cat a double dose of petting and he will understand that you acted in his best interest.

Cats, like all other animals, occasionally misbehave. There are several acceptable disciplines in training a cat, but the first rule concerns prompt response time. If disciplinary action is to work, it must be administered immediately, or your cat will not relate the punishment to the crime. If you pick up your cat regularly to hold and pet him but sometimes pick him up to chastise him long after the fact, your cat will be confused and grow to fear and resent you.

Your goal is to get your cat to respond to a sharply voiced "No!" To teach him what that "No!" means, use any or all of the following methods. A sudden clap of the hands along with a firmly spoken "No!" often startles him enough to arrest bad behavior. If aural reprimands are not working, use a surprise squirt of water from a spray bottle, atomizer, or water pistol, again incorporated with a sharply spoken "No!" For those really stubborn problems, a swift, firm rap across the nose with the tip of your fingers is permissible, but remember to include that "No!" Your cat will find each of these approaches unpleasant, but no physical harm is incurred and certainly no pain is involved. Eventually, he will associate the hand clap, spray, and nose tap with your "No!" and you will get prompt response on the word alone.

By the way, don't bother to point toward any cat-created problem and expect your cat to look where you are pointing. He will look directly at your finger, not what you are pointing at. Pointing works only if your finger is actually touching what you wish your cat to observe.

With these basics firmly in hand, let's proceed to specific problems and solutions. Although it's impossible to cover all situations your cat might create, you should be able to form an effective response to most problems from these samples.

Problem: Scratching the Furniture
Solution: In the long run, our specially designed scratching pad (described in Chapter 6) is the best answer, but if you are not there to pick up your cat and take him to the scratching pad—or if he has not yet learned to use it regularly—try the following remedies.

Chances are, a chair or sofa is getting scratched. Attach a sheet of aluminum foil so it covers the spot being ripped at. The unexpected sound and surface will frighten your cat and keep him away. If the arm of a chair or couch is a favorite target, set a trap. Hang a spare piece of cloth down over the scratching place, secured lightly by a paperback book balanced on the top or horizontal part of the armrest. When your cat reaches up and scratches, the cloth will be pulled down—along with the book. Boom! Result: one scared cat who no longer likes the arm of that chair. . . .

You may also place a dish of diluted white vinegar under the couch or chair. What functions as a mild room deodorizer for you acts as an effective deterrent to your finicky cat's nose.

Of course, when you catch kitty in the act, use the discipline techniques discussed earlier and take him immediately to his scratching pad.

Problem: Chewing and Biting
Solution: Like scratching, chewing and biting are instinctive for cats, particularly for teething kittens. If you keep the proper toys around, there will be no need for your cat

to chew inappropriate things—like furniture, curtains, electric cords, or even your fingers. But if your cat does chew on cords, rub them with Tabasco sauce, white vinegar mixed with water, or lemon juice. If your cat likes to chew on your fingers and you don't think it's amusing, rub lemon juice on your hands and let your cat get a taste of that. If it's a table leg being gnawed (or anything that one of these liquid deterrents might damage), try sprinkling a little black pepper around the area. One sniff and . . . achoo! No more cat teething there.

If you would prefer not to use one of these deterrents for any reason, keep a spray bottle filled with water nearby and watch carefully. Avoid commercial spray repellents; some of them leave a residue or stain you can avoid with plain water. And always remember to use your cat's name when you discipline him.

Problem: Soiling Away from the Litter Box
Solution: If you are absolutely sure your cat is properly litter trained and you have made certain he has no physical disorder (see Chapter 10 for more details), try moving his food to the spot where he has soiled. Cats are fastidious and will not eat where they relieve themselves. After a few days you should be able to move the food back to its normal place. This technique is discussed in full in Chapter 5. If you are unable to correct this behavior quickly, however, take your cat to your vet for a complete checkup; he could be telling you he's ill. But remember, always make sure your cat's litter box is fresh and clean first.

Problem: Using Off-Limits Areas
Solution: To help define areas you wish to make out of bounds, you must give your cat a special place of his own, so when you use a discipline technique to get him away

from your space, he has a secure and pleasant alternative. Cats like to sleep in a warm, soft, sheltered area, and once they have discovered their own special place, they stick with it. You can turn your cat's territorial instincts to your advantage by creating a bed for your cat near or even on top of whatever you wish to protect. Find a box or basket about twice the size of your cat and cover the surface with a blanket or pillow. Try using a blanket or pillow your cat already likes to increase your chances of success. This new bed will protect the surface you are worried about while allowing your cat to stay in more or less the same spot.

Once your cat gets used to his new bed, you can, if you wish, attempt to move it. Good places to put this new bed: near a heat source, by a sunny window, under a low table. Take your cat there repeatedly. Introduce new toys and bring him old favorite ones there; do whatever you can to get your cat to spend time in it. When the new bed and area start to smell like the cat's old place, he will be more likely to accept them and make them part of his rightful territory. Hint: Be sneaky! Move your cat there while he is sleeping.

If you do not succeed in establishing a cat-bed location of your choice, don't feel like you have failed an important test of wills. Sleep is a cat's main activity and something cats are most particular about. You may not be able to change your cat's sleeping habits, but you can at least keep him away from improper places. If you must, chase your cat off the sacred couch, that antique chair, your heirloom quilt—until he settles on a place of mutual consent. After all, you *have* given him a bed to lie in.

Problem: Plant Eating
Solution: People think of cats as hunters, and therefore as exclusively carnivorous. But in the wild and at home, fe-

lines do like—and need—to eat green plants. If your cat is chewing on *your* houseplants, he could be needing greens for dietary reasons. Check with your vet to see if there is any physical problem your cat may be trying to correct by instinctively searching out green plants to eat. If he does need greens, grow your cat his own garden! Most pet stores carry the kinds of seeds and plants your cat will enjoy. Look especially for long grasses and even homegrown catnip, which is entirely legal. Grow them by your cat's favorite resting spots if possible, but by all means do *not* grow them anywhere near the plants you want your cat to leave alone. Kitty will never understand the difference between plant A and plant B.

As for protecting your plants, they should be hardy enough to survive being sprayed with diluted white vinegar, or lemon juice or alcohol—effective not only in keeping your cat away and your plants from becoming kitty salad, but also in keeping your plants free of many bugs and diseases. Also try sprinkling ground black pepper around your plant dishes. And don't forget: if you see your cat at this undesirable activity, the spray bottle is very effective. And your plants will thank you doubly for the moisture!

For cats who tend to dig up potting soil, put good-sized pebbles on the surface of the soil, so digging becomes more of a pain than a pleasure.

Finally, stay on the safe side and keep poisonous plants out of your house and yard.

Some Final Tips

Some bad behavior is caused through misunderstanding. For example, if you have given your cat a sock for a toy, he is apt to consider all socks toys. Keep the laundry out of harm's way and you won't need to confuse kitty by punishing him for playing with the wrong sock. Try to think like a cat. Your cat can't think like a human.

After a bit of strict discipline, always pick up your cat for some nice petting and scratching. There should never be an end to reestablishing the bond of trust and affection between you and your cat.

You are sure to have problems other than those we have covered, but the basic idea behind proper cat discipline holds true in all situations: be consistent, determined, and untiring. And finally, before you scold, evaluate your cat's behavior. Is your cat really misbehaving? Or is he merely asking you to play with him? Don't forget that you are the center of your cat's life. Make time to spend with him.

In the next chapter, we'll explore problems requiring a touch of finesse. It's a finishisng course of fine points for cats called "Etikitty."

4
Etikitty

We've started you and your cat on the road to a long and satisfying relationship. Strict discipline was emphasized as we looked at situations where right and wrong ruled the day. But we know there is more to any relationship than what can be laid out carefully in black and white; there are those gray areas. Here we will help you go deeper into your cat's personality and become familiar with its finer points.

On a social level, many aspects of human behavior—when to stand, when to shake hands, how to kiss Auntie on the cheek, etc.—are *second* nature to us. This means that although we hardly have to think about them, we were not born with these behavior patterns—we have *learned* them. Our cats need to be taught some social graces too.

To keep your cat's behavior within the guidelines you have chosen, you must remember that once you have set the ground rules, you must stick to them. The consistency of your cat's behavior depends entirely upon the consistency of your disciplinary example.

Let's accompany your cat through a normal day. We start in the wee hours of the morning . . .

A cat's internal alarm clock goes off with uncanny precision. It is controlled by two stimuli: sunshine and hunger. You may find that your morning schedule clashes violently with your cat's. What do you do?

Cats can be terribly persistent, which can make them useful as living alarm clocks. The trick is learning how to set them. To bring out this ability in your cat, feed him something he is particularly fond of as soon as you get up. He will quickly associate *your* rising with *his* eating.

Once this pattern is established, you can adjust the wake-up call to your desired hour. Decide what time you wish to get up and be consistent. Your cat will try to get you up earlier and earlier at first. But simply ignore kitty until you feel it's time to arise. Do not give in. Resist all tricks, meows, and pawings! When absolutely necessary, push your cat away. But stay put. Soon your cat will learn to wait until the proper hour, and his biological clock will adjust permanently. You'll find this much sweeter than any bell, buzzer, or radio alarm.

On the debit side, your cat does not understand weekends or holidays. You will have created an alarm clock that sets itself automatically every night. Also remember that your cat does not comprehend daylight savings time and must be taught to "spring forward, fall back." So think about the long-term consequences before you proceed in teaching your cat to get you up. But we think you'll love it.

If you don't wish to be awakened by your cat, never feed him first thing in the morning. Make feeding the *last* thing you do before you leave the house. If your cat insists on trying to get you up, resolutely ignore him. Do not even make eye contact. Save pushing him away as a last resort because he may think you want to play games. Pretend your cat does not exist until you are ready to face the world. This should only take a week or so with even the most stubborn of cats. If you really want to be left alone until you've had your coffee, offer no petting, scratching, conversation. Nothing! If there is one thing a cat understands, it's a stone wall.

Now you and your cat are up and about. Don't forget to open all of your drapes. Your cat likes the sun as much or more than you do. Cats claw away at things because of their needs to stretch and scratch. But they are especially interested in drapes because behind those drapes lies the sun—and the possibility of discovering favorite sunny places to lie in. Use Chapter 6 as a guide to avoiding scratching problems by giving your cat permissible alternative scratching sites, but remember to open your drapes regularly. This could make drape clawing something your cat will never even begin to learn.

Our day continues and we go to the bathroom and find kitty drinking out of the toilet bowl. Yuck! Actually, there is nothing particularly unhealthy or unsanitary about this habit *if* you maintain a clean toilet bowl. However, if you use an automatic-dispensing chemical bowl cleaner—or simply disapprove of cats on the toilet for reasons of aesthetics—you should keep your cat away from the bowl. Also, if you wish to attempt "The Flush Alternative" described in Chapter 5, you must not allow this drinking pattern to become habitual. The most practical way to halt it is always to keep the seat *and* lid closed. Simple, of course, but you are not the only person who is ever going to use the toilet! If someone else forgets to put the lid down and you find your cat drinking from the bowl, pick him up, say "No!" firmly, and then carry him to his feeding station and refill the water bowl with fresh, cool water. Always keep plenty of fresh water readily available for your cat. Change it every day, regardless of how much is left.

It is afternoon and along come some visitors. How will your cat react? If you have ever seen a cat who lives in a small store, you know that cats can respond well to strangers and are not as aloof as their reputation makes them out to be. Store cats tend to be calm and friendly toward the whole world. Everyone who comes in seems pleased just to look at them, and a few may give them a brief pat. Why are these cats so well adjusted to unknown people?

There is really no great secret about this. From their infancy, store cats spend their lives in the company of . . . well, company. Strangers, new visitors, and a good-sized work staff are part of their routine. It's unlikely you want to turn your house into a store, but you should go out of your way to introduce your cat to everyone who comes to your home. Make it part of your cat's routine. Include plumbers, delivery boys, cookie-selling girl scouts, and friends who are regular visitors. This is a perfect time for reinforcing your cat's name training. Have all these different folks use your cat's name. That way, you can be sure your cat is responding to the sound of his name, not the sound of your voice. This is particularly important for those times when your cat must be left with the vet or at the kennel or in the care of a friend when you are away on vacation.

Allow your guests to pet your cat. Encourage it. Give special tips about where he likes to be scratched. Behind the ear, for example, under the chin, high on his back, or wherever he likes best. After this introduction (we are now talking about your friends; we hope the plumber has gone to work!) put your cat down and let him make some decisions on his own. Your guest may have the scent of other animals from other homes, and this may either intrigue or displease your cat, but it shouldn't unduly upset him. At worst, he will merely retreat to another room. And that's okay.

If your cat stays in the room with you and your guest, start a simple game with him and let your guest take over. This can also help put a noncat-lover at ease. Nothing more complicated than yarn chasing or rolling a small toy is called for. After all, your visitor came to see you, not your cat.

Throughout the day, your cat may attempt to interrupt your regular activities. Not by getting into trouble exactly, but by just being a nuisance, pacing back and forth near an off-limits area, crying for no discernible reason, constantly getting in the way. He is probably suffering from acute restlessness. It is especially common in indoor apartment cats. Chances are, all these actions are your cat's way of attracting and keeping your attention. This is how your cat talks to you and, to be specific, complains to you.

If you have the time to play, that is the best response. But if you are not in the mood or don't have the time to play, make sure your cat has some healthy, acceptable outlets for these feline feelings of restlessness. Open a closet door and you will create a small adventure for him as he explores new territory. (No china cabinets, please.) An open drawer can make an interesting place for ambush. Open a window and create a cat porch—but make sure any window you open is well screened for safety. Cats are wonderful leapers, but they can misjudge their probable landing sites. And contrary to popular belief, cats *do not* always land on their feet. Safety first, last, and always! Bring out a new toy or reintroduce an old one into your cat's life. The one thing *not* to do is to allow your lack of interest to lead your cat to start using any off-limits area. If you do, it won't be off limits for long!

Dinner for you and dinner for your cat should be two separate affairs. Combine them at your own risk. Keeping your cat off the dinner table and away from lowly begging are best accomplished with the stern disciplinary techniques discussed in Chapter 3. A loud "No!", hand claps, and the spray bottle can all be applied as needed.

If your cat is a true gourmet who must taste some of your fine cuisine *and* if you wish to share a bit, fix a small plate and serve it to your cat at his regular feeding station. It is best to do this after *your* meal is over. Your cat will learn to wait his turn and not be too obstreperous through your mealtime. To ensure a peaceful dinner hour, you might try feeding the cat his usual dinner first—he'll then be full and satisfied and hence less interested in your food.

With dinner over, you have time at last to get to the morning newspaper you've been waiting all day to read, or perhaps a fat luxurious novel, when . . . PLOP! Seated directly in your sight line is your furry friend. "How does he always know exactly what article I am reading and manage to cover just *that* one?" Move your cat over. He obviously wants your attention and may be satisfied just to be near you. If kitty keeps climbing back, give him a toy. He'll get the message if you merely insist and stand up (sometimes literally) for your own rights.

At last, the day draws to a close. Just as you are about to drift off to sleep . . . CRASH! The garbage can has been tipped over. Here *you* must take some responsibility. Discarded chicken bones are simply too tempting (and bone splinters can be dangerous to your cat as well). Don't play the devil: take that garbage out *before* trouble occurs. It is normal instinct for any cat to seek out food, and it is almost impossible to train a cat *not* to follow a delicious scent to its source.

If this habit is so strongly established that your cat will tip over the garbage regardless of a lack of interesting items in there, stop him cold by decorating the can with a few inflated balloons. Most cats do not like balloons. If they swipe at one, it is liable to pop and scare them away from this "bad" place for good.

General cat-proofing of your house can be accomplished the same way child-proofing is. Lock up dangerous and fragile things and do not leave temptations out and about. Never leave meat unattended. Make sure there is strong wire or plastic mesh over electric fans. Think about the places your cat can leap to (something you don't need to worry about when child-proofing a home). Keep medicine inside properly secured cabinets. Don't leave those antique glass and crystal pieces in harm's way. Make sure all knobs and latches within reach are too tight for a cat to maneuver.

But the best care you can give your cat is to treat him like a friend. Talk to your cat. Yes, talk. He may not understand what you are saying, but he will respond to the sound of your voice, its pace and various tones. Besides, it's companionable for both of you. *You* must set the example: the better your manners toward your cat, the better your cat's manners will be.

Congratulations, you have made it through the day. You, and your cat.

5

Litter Training and the Flush Alternative

One of the easiest tasks for the new owner of a kitten is toilet training. In most cases, observing Mama has made this delicate task already complete upon your adoption of the kitten. You may simply introduce your cat to his new litter box and be done with this assignment.

Watch your cat for the first few days to be sure no problems arise. You may need to remind him of the location and purpose of the litter box by picking him up and gently placing him inside it. Take his front paw and give him a brief demonstration in litter digging. He *will* get the idea. Cats instinctively bury their waste so as not to leave a telltale scent for their enemies. A few owner-initiated trips are probably all your cat will need.

Still, there can be complications. But there *are* ways to clean up any problems you might encounter.

Is your cat refusing to use his box? Try these remedies. Keep the litter box clean. People who have a basement often maintain their cat's facility downstairs and—after a

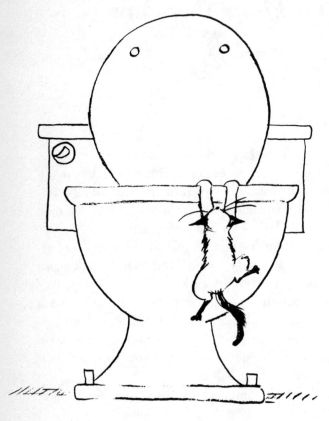

CANEMAKER

month of neglect—are amazed when kitty despoils their Oriental rug. Try to clean out your cat's box at least every other day. This job need not be too offensive. In fact, the more often you do it, the less offensive it is. Any large, slotted kitchen spoon will do the job nicely, but you may purchase a special kitty pooper scooper at your local pet shop instead. This device also makes it easy to stir the litter so it has a chance to dry out. Besides keeping the box more appealing to your cat, this will greatly prolong the life of your litter.

Still, litter will not last forever! Two or three weeks is about all it can take. Less time than that if you have more than one cat. Out with the old, in with the new. Cat litter is available in a mind-boggling assortment of textures, materials, and scents, but plain ground clay is the cheapest and best choice. If your cat spends much of his time out of doors, he may well prefer a neighbor's garden to an indoor box. Then your litter could last indefinitely.

Now, if your cat is *still* soiling in an unacceptable spot, try this approach. Cats are discriminating animals, so appeal to their scruples. When you have located the general area your cat feels is a perfect toilet facility but you insist works better as a living room, turn that spot into a temporary feeding station. Cats refuse to eat where they relieve themselves. Introduce your cat to his new food station with something absolutely delicious in it. After the cat has supped, show him a beautifully fresh litter box far away from the point of contention. Place him in the box and give him some nice scratches under the chin. Every hour or so take him back to the properly located litter facilities and . . . Voila! Your cat's behavior will be corrected.

After a few days, you will be able to return the feeding trays and dishes to a more appropriate location. But play fair! Do not ignore your litter box! Keep it clean and reasonably dry. Your cat will appreciate it and in the long run, so will you.

If, despite all efforts, your cat is still urinating anyplace that pleases him, you may have an unhealthy animal on your hands. A trip to the vet is called for. But do not confuse sexual spraying in male cats with bad toilet habits. It is an entirely different problem. The strong odor, often accompanied by altered behavior, will alert you to this situation. Details on alleviating this problem are covered in Chapter 10.

And now, a few pages for the adventurous . . .

The Flush Alternative

Simply put, many (but not all) cats can be taught to use a human-style flush toilet. Fortunately, they haven't the strength to do their own flushing, or this delightful game could quadruple your water bills!

Once a cat begins a bowel movement, he must complete it. Some owners we know have used this knowledge as a basis for training their cat to use a toilet. By watching the cat's litter habits, they come to recognize the distinctive high-arched back position a cat holds while making a bowel movement. Then, during the movement, the owner swoops down, lifts the cat, and places him on the toilet seat. Some of the drawbacks to this system: teaching the cat toilet seat balance at such a delicate moment, your cat's resentment at being disturbed from his business, the mess in attempting this during urination, and the need for the owner to be home throughout these training procedures to guard the litter box.

Our method allows your cat to *teach himself* this toilet

seat maneuver. You maintain your role as supervisor, not taskmaster.

Owners who leave their cats unattended for days at a time often find that a clean, open toilet bowl is a favorite watering trough for their cat. If you are one of these owners, do not attempt this toilet-training technique. But if you have a good deal of patience and determination, you may find that the following steps can turn your cat's litter box into an ancient relic.

The first step is to acquire a litter box sturdy enough and sized properly to hold a standard toilet seat. Place it immediately next to the real toilet. Many apartment owners find this is the natural location for the litter box anyway, as it makes daily scooping convenient to a perfect disposal unit—and reminds them of their duty to keep the box as clean as any cat could wish.

Now go to a store that sells discount hardware and purchase the cheapest hard toilet seat you can find. Remove the lid portion so you are left with only the part that is actually used for sitting. Place it on top of the litter box and wait about a month while your cat gets used to its being there.

At first, your cat may attempt to ignore the presence of this plastic intrusion and take care of his business within the tightly constricted confines of the toilet seat hole. But in due time, as kitty becomes too big to get *into* the hole, he will find it more comfortable to sit *on* the seat. If your cat is having trouble figuring out what the seat is for, place him on it (in the correct direction and position) and give him a good scratch under the chin. Approve of this perch as often as you can. Try occasionally to watch your cat for any progress. You may wish to compliment kitty on a fine sense of balance.

When your cat has been sitting on the toilet seat reg-

ularly (for at least two weeks), begin *slowly* raising the seat,
using bricks or pieces of wood to support it. If you are the
slightest bit handy, we recommend a log cabin–style building pattern. Simply use one-half-inch- to one-inch–thick
pieces of wood, two at a time, and crisscross your way up
week by week, alternating the position of the added wood
by placing it on the north-south sides one week, east-west
the next, then back to north-south, and so on (see Diagram
A). You can stabilize this structure by securing the toilet
seat to the first elevation with some strong tape. Nail each
additional level to the previous one as you add it on. This
method also creates a barrier so your cat can not go *under*
the seat and *into* the litter box. Make sure the toilet seat is
firmly balanced at all levels. Any tipping or unsteadiness
will send you back promptly to step one.

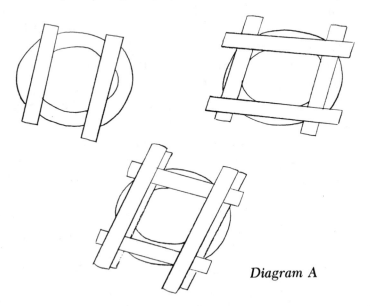

Diagram A

Once the raising of the seat has begun, proceed at the
rate of about one inch per week. *Do not allow your cat to*

observe this maneuver! Your cat can deal more easily with the thought that the ground is sinking than that his human companion is making life difficult for some unfathomable reason!

You should skip a week of raising occasionally, to make sure kitty has a chance to adjust to the higher elevation, but the goal is eventually to reach the exact height of the neighboring toilet (see Diagram B). Depending on your cat, the whole progression may take anywhere from three to six months. If it seems to be taking considerably longer, you may wish to give up on this one. But don't blame yourself or your cat. The flush alternative is not for everyone.

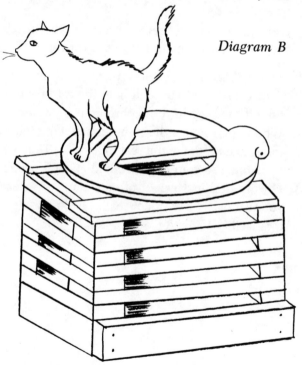

Diagram B

For those of you still with us, however, . . .

When kitty's toilet seat has been at the same level as the

real toilet seat for a few days, the time is ripe for swift action! Without letting your cat see what is going on, remove the training toilet seat, the bricks and/or wood, *and* the litter box.

While you're relaxing in a far corner of your home, your cat is most perplexed. Do not yield to temptation and spend hours waiting and watching for the great moment. Leave your cat to make his own discovery. Almost all cats who get this far go on to make the real toilet seat connection. And the next time you enter your bathroom, there may well be a little surprise awaiting you.

Congratulations!

Haven't quite gotten there, but still determined? Here are three additional tips to help your cat reach the goal.

1. At the final stage of elevation, substitute water for your cat's litter. This will help the cat become accustomed to going to the bathroom over water.
2. When you remove the training box, tape the training toilet seat on top of the real toilet seat. This piece will be familiar to your cat and could make the difference.
3. During the final weeks of elevation, occasionally sit your cat on the real toilet seat so he knows he can use this facility too and won't be afraid of it.

6
Sanity versus Claws

Cats come about as near to perfect household guests as any creatures in the animal kingdom (including human relatives), but even a cat is not entirely without failings. Topping the list for most people is a cat's tendency to scratch wherever—and whatever—he pleases. One friend insists her cat has a natural talent as a furniture appraiser, proven beyond doubt by kitty's selection of the finest antique pieces as favorite scratching posts.

Can this scratching problem be controlled?

Must cats scratch?

The answer to both of these questions is yes. There are three main reasons for this damaging habit. Understanding them can help you deal with the problem more effectively. Keep in mind that the training goal is not to eliminate scratching, but to redirect this *necessary* activity toward what *you* consider acceptable terrain.

The infant kitten enters the world and makes his first decision: let's eat. Getting hold of an open teat is quickly

accomplished (often with a helpful nudge from Mama), and the flow of milk is aided when the kitten begins a treading action with his paws.

This treading or kneading action becomes a permanent part of the cat's behavior. It can be observed in the adult cat as he settles down for a nap or during a lap session with a human friend. As the cat treads, his claws penetrate whatever surface lies below. Is it a sofa cushion? A stomach? A favorite quilt? Your kneecap? They are all mother's milk to your cat.

The bad news: this treading action can be stopped only at the moment of occurrence by carrying your cat to an area you consider risk-free. The good news: damage accrued through treading action is minimal. Those who find even minor damage unbearable may wish to consider declawing or nail clipping, discussed in detail later on in this chapter.

The second damaging activity is the body stretch. One of the pure aesthetic pleasures in owning a cat is watching the elegance he maintains throughout his daily activities. Anyone with an eye for beauty delights at the sight of a cat performing his customary body stretch upon waking in the morning or rising from a short catnap. Problems occur when those forepaws reach far ahead and the claws grab hold of anything convenient—like your authentic Persian throw rug—to serve as an anchor. During the stretch, the claws are apt to get stuck. In his efforts to extricate himself, your cat may pull, twist, or even shred your carpet or cushion.

Stretching is a natural way for a cat to work out kinks in his muscles, and it helps restore circulation quickly to the extremities. The damage that results from the body stretch can be controlled only by clipping or declawing the cat. But most owners find the damage to be sporadic and minor and something most can easily live with.

The third and most aggressively destructive clawing pattern is the repeated scratching your cat performs to mark out his territory and help groom his nails, keeping them hard and sharp. You may occasionally come upon an entire, well-shaped claw "shell" that has been shed in the grooming process. This is perfectly natural. You want to encourage your cat to take proper care of himself, yet you can't allow him to destroy household treasures.

Constant and prolonged scratching causes considerable damage and can easily turn into an unpleasant bone of contention between you and your cat. Even owners who are able to let their cats outside regularly find this habit a problem. You cannot teach a cat the value of new upholstery, and you should not try to keep a cat from maintaining healthy grooming habits—or from his natural instinctive behavior. Although a loud hand clap or a quick spritz of water from an atomizer or water pistol will stop scratching in most on-the-spot situations, who can tell what may be going on when you are not around to catch the culprit?!

Scratching posts are one of the most popular accessories for cats, yet they rarely function as well as they should. Why is this? Perhaps it is because of their vertical structure. The people who design these posts have watched cats out of doors and have made an imitation tree for the cat to scratch on while *inside* the house. But watch your cat when he is being particularly destructive: chances are, his position will be more horizontal than vertical. So we shall build a scratching post your cat will actually use—one that lies flat upon the ground, perfectly suited to your cat's natural scratching inclinations. If you place this pad in one of kitty's favorite observing spots he will be more inclined to seek it out for scratching and for watching his world from his *own* seat. Your cat can spend time *on* his post, making it part of his territory, hence a wonderful place to scratch.

Here's how.

Find a topless box large enough to comfortably accommodate your cat—perhaps eight inches wide and a good two feet in length. Bind together strips of corrugated cardboard that match the size and depth of the box, with the corrugated edges facing up (see Diagram A). When you fit the cardboard into the box, you have completed your scratching pad (see Diagram B). As simple as that!

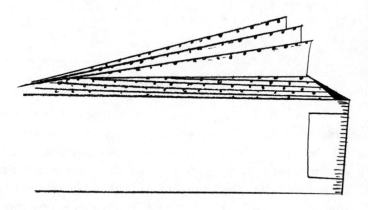

Diagram A

Now for the training.

If you see your cat scratching anywhere other than on his scratching pad—even if it's a place of little concern to you—pick kitty up gently and place him in the center of the pad. Take his paws and start the scratching movement. When he starts to scratch of his own accord, tell him what a fine cat he is and calmly stroke his back. Not enough to distract him, just to reassure him. If you find your cat needs a little extra incentive, sprinkle a small amount of catnip on the pad. The catnip will fall between the corrugation and provide a good reason for your cat to scratch right there!

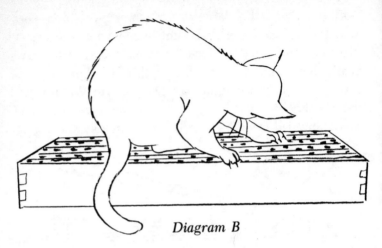

Diagram B

As with all training procedures, this one takes some time, and you may never entirely cure your cat of scratching elsewhere. But a well-used pad *can* significantly decrease damage to the rest of your house. Be aware that taking your cat to the scratching pad will not be effective in controlling treading or stretching. Your cat won't comprehend any connection between those activities and a scratching pad. A good stretch is no fun in a two-foot-long box—and who wants to "milk" corrugated cardboard!

You can also keep your cat's claws clipped. It is fairly easy to do, but be sure to do it with the proper equipment. The clippers (carried by most pet stores) must be sharp enough to give a clean, quick break. If you have to struggle to clip the nail, your clippers are not sharp enough, and you may damage the nail bed. Gently squeeze your cat's paw to expose each nail and clip off only the offending tip. Clip *only* the tip, the translucent white part. Avoid the pinkish-colored quick. If you feel particularly gun-shy about this, ask your vet to let you watch a sample clipping before forging ahead yourself.

Declawing is almost always safe and effective when the claws (front only) are properly removed by a good veterinarian. Declawing does require general anesthesia, and entails the risk of any major surgery, but your cat will adjust to his new clawless state within a week or two and will suffer no psychological behavioral changes. Your cat's scratching is instinctive, and will continue even after he has been declawed.

If you are thinking of declawing an older cat, you should note that recovering from major surgery becomes more difficult as any living thing grows older. But it is rarely any more difficult to adjust psychologically for a cat who has had his claws for twelve years than it is for one who has had them for only two. One cat we are particularly fond of still hunts as successfully as he did before his claws were removed at age six. He recently brought home a small rabbit! Look, ma, no claws! Cats who *must* live primarily outdoors, however, should never be declawed.

We do not recommend declawing for all or even most cats. But if you feel this must be done to keep you and your cat on speaking terms in your house, there is no reason to be miserably guilty about it every time you watch your cat scratching furiously away *without* those damaging claws. He is not aware of the change, and a declawed cat *is* better than a homeless one.

7
The Path of Leash Resistance

The training methods and ideas discussed in this book go hand in hand with a cat's natural instincts and are designed to work *with* your cat's personality. You were probably surprised at the range of possibilities, and may have been unaware of many things a cat likes to do (or perhaps were previously unable to make your cat do them), but nothing has gone against the grain of a cat's natural behavior. Until now. Leash training is different.

In the great outdoors, your cat stops being just your pet and becomes an explorer, a hunter, and the hunted, all at the same time. Combine this with his inborn physical ability to run, leap, and climb, and the concept of walking on a lead along a relatively confined path on the ground is obviously unnatural for your cat. Still, behaving properly on a leash is possible, given training, and is a necessary skill a cat must acquire in our modern, mobile society.

You must teach your cat to behave on a leash for his own safety. Whether or not he will take to this discipline and want to walk on the leash for fun will be more your cat's decision than yours. Some cats, particularly indoor city cats, love the opportunity to go out of doors. Your time and patience will be called upon in training, but it is imperative for all cats to learn at least to *accept* a leash when it becomes a necessity.

Trips to your veterinarian may be the most obvious instance of the need to place your cat on a leash. But just as important are your vacations (even if kitty doesn't take the cruise, he'll have to head for a kennel), and other journeys outside your home with your cat. If you use a transport box, you must be prepared for the moment when your cat comes out into new surroundings. There is no way to predict what his reaction will be. Only a leash offers you the assurance of control.

Many cat owners tell us their cats trust them so well they can simply hold them in their arms and have complete control. What these owners forget is that they cannot maintain control of the variables that may surprise, intrigue, or frighten their cats. How will your cat react to other animals at your vet's, or to a loud street noise? Once outside your house, your cat himself will not know how he will respond to new stimuli, so how can *you* know? So please, no matter how close you are with your pet, use a leash at all times when transporting kitty.

Here are some tools you will need. We recommend a figure-eight–style nylon harness with a lead attached to it (see Diagram A). The pressure points inherent in this type of restrainer will neither hurt your cat nor obstruct his normal body movements (although your cat may stage an Academy Award–winning performance to make you think otherwise).

A traditional neck collar and lead can also be used with

Diagram A

success, but only on the most willing of subjects. Many cats regularly wear neck collars for flea protection or identification purposes and are comfortable with them. A good test for proper fit with any neck collar is to allow room for two fingers to slip comfortably under the collar without producing breathing discomfort for your cat. Even with a properly fitted collar, the added tension from the lead can cause discomfort and a struggle. If your cat resists, it will only cause frustration for him and for you. Sometimes the cat wins and manages to slip right out of the collar. Making the collar tighter does not help! And it can hurt your cat or cause breathing problems. In an extreme case, the collar can get stuck between the back of your cat's head and his mouth. Keeping all this in mind, if you still feel that a neck collar is right for your cat, first make sure that you find one with variable loop size, which allows a reasonable compromise between too tight and too loose. And never use a dog-style choke collar.

A third choice, surprisingly, is a standard piece of dog equipment. Dogs are often walked on a leash attached to a separate harness, which offers superb control. If you can find a harness like this that is small enough, light enough, and *pliable* enough for a cat, you might wish to try it. But please take great care to see where and how it puts pressure on your cat. The advantage with this kind of harness is that the harness is a separate component and your cat can wear it around the house. He can take his time getting to feel comfortable with it, if you are having trouble getting him used to wearing anything. Since this kind of harness can be worn without a lead, the cat does not need to be under your supervision at all times. Never allow a cat to wander unattended with any kind of lead or leash attached to his collar or harness because it can catch on various objects. Even if the cat isn't hurt by it, your house will soon be a shambles.

Now, on with the training.

Choose a lead—make sure it is not too heavy—and attach it to the harness of your choice. Check carefully to see where it pulls on your cat's body when you gently tug it in various directions. Use the previously mentioned "two-finger" test at each point of contact with your cat. This procedure is easier if done by two people: one who pulls gently on the leash and another who feels for pressure points on kitty.

Now take off the harness and apply pressure with your hand and fingers on the same spots where the harness was pulling. Your cat's reaction will quickly tell you if you are causing him actual discomfort and possible danger. Make sure you take the harness off before you check for problems. If the harness is still on, kitty may make the connection and pretend that it hurts. A cat can astound his owner with intelligence when it suits his purpose.

As in all training, it is important to choose a proper time for initiation. When introducing the leash, avoid those times when your cat is in a particularly active mood. On the other hand, don't wake him up in an attempt to sneak the harness on. The best times are when your cat is calmly sitting or lying down but is alert and watching your activities.

While putting on the harness, pet your cat and talk gently to him. You may need to restrain curious or defensive paws, but if you have established a sense of trust between yourself and your pet, you should have no problems. If you have not established good trust, you are never going to get your cat to walk with you anyway. You may need to work on your relationship by referring to our earlier chapters.

As soon as you have gotten the harness on (see Diagram B), watch closely for your cat's initial reaction. There are three general responses.

Diagram B

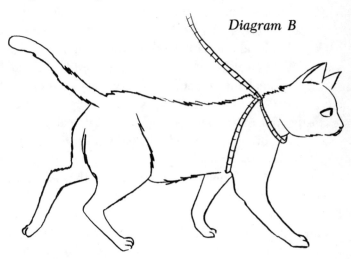

Our first cat wants nothing to do with any of this. This cat will most likely dash away, become skittish, and roll about trying to get the harness off. This cat should be picked up and held reassuringly. Remember always to support your cat with one arm around him and a hand on the bottom under his legs and the other arm holding him in front, the hand held high on his back. When the cat calms down, place him back on the floor while you hold the lead up and out of the way so it is not dragging behind and annoying him. Don't attempt to do anything too soon with this cat. Simply spend a bit of time (about ten minutes) once or twice a day getting him used to the idea of wearing this contraption. When he starts to relax on the leash, you may wish to use food treats to reinforce good behavior, but never use them to "correct" bad behavior. Your cat will quickly see that bad behavior is a way to get a treat! What's more, he may confuse what's expected of him with what he can earn a treat for.

Cat number two mistakenly believes the harness and leash are some kind of punishment (a kitty stockade) for improper behavior. This cat will look depressed: ears laid back on his head and crouched low to the ground, as if to say, "What have I done this time, master?" A pathetic sight! But this kind of reaction is fairly easy to alter. Bring out a few of the cat's favorite toys and start to play as if the leash did not exist. (Of course, you must make sure the leash does not get entangled.) To help get this cat started, you may have to lift his belly off the floor gently with your hand or foot. In general, let him know that all kinds of normal activities are possible while he wears a harness and lead.

Our last cat will certainly please a few lucky owners, as he will not be fazed in the least by wearing a leash. Such a cat will go about his daily functions in the most natural of ways. If you're the lucky owner, immediately pick up the lead and walk a few paces to and fro. Allow the cat to direct you, at first, in whatever direction takes his fancy. The idea is to let him make the connection between the harness and walking about. Such a wonder cat may advance quickly to walk training and may skip the two-week period of adjustment to wearing the harness and lead.

But for the rest of you . . .

Once you are certain that the harness fits properly, it is time to get your cat used to wearing it with a lead. Start on an evening when you know you can remain undisturbed with your cat for a solid chunk of time. Then daily, for two weeks, keep your cat in his walking gear for at least ten minutes at a time. You needn't do anything at first, except be around to make sure your cat does not get into trouble with the lead. You are waiting and watching for your cat to just "be himself," but with the harness and lead on. When your cat begins to walk, leap, play, and perhaps even eat while harnessed, you may start teaching him to walk with you.

Always bear in mind that walking on a lead with you setting the general direction and pace is not part of your cat's instinctive behavior. You must consistently praise and encourage your cat with petting, scratches, and cuddling.

Start by walking in the house. While holding the leash, let your cat walk toward something of interest, like dinner or a favorite toy. Keep these initial walks quite short, or your cat will think he is being punished. As long as his tail and ears remain fairly erect, you will know your cat is not misconstruing this exercise as forced labor. When you notice unhappiness, stop. Drop the lead and wait until your cat relaxes before making another attempt. This may take a little while, but be patient, and always be sure each session ends on a happy note.

Here are a few tips for especially difficult cats. To get

him going, try nudging kitty gently from behind with your foot. Or slip your foot under his belly and let him "ride" for a few paces with his feet just touching the floor. Some people use a stick for nudging and lifting, but this can be threatening to your cat. You may try the two-person approach, with one person on the lead and the other on the floor, encouraging and coaxing the cat. The person on the floor may actually move your cat's legs to instill the idea of walking. Or he might use a food treat, held just out of reach, to get those first steps taken.

As you continue these sessions and your cat stops viewing the leash as a threat, your indoor walks should get progressively longer and cover more distance. But if your cat refuses to take a single step, don't feel as though all your time and effort has been wasted. The important lesson is teaching your cat to *accept* being on a leash and in a harness so you can maintain control should your cat panic and try to leap away during a necessary trip out of the house.

Those of you with adventurous cats who are responding well thus far can now move on to advanced training for outdoor walking. Begin by taking your cat for brief jaunts outside the house while you hold him in your arms. Cats are always aware of their environment, and a few trips in your arms will allow them to take in sights and sounds new to their experience. It will also pique their curiosity. Remember to have the harness and lead on your cat during these "getting acquainted" strolls so he begins to aciate this gear with the great outdoors. It will probably take two or three walks before your cat feels confident enough to stand on his own four feet and think about his first steps forward.

On your fourth or fifth excursion—or whenever you feel

your cat is ready (head held high and looking inquisitive, not crouched and buried in your arms)—place him on the ground just before you reach the entrance to your house. Your cat should recognize the sight and smell of it by now and will naturally walk toward the door as you follow, holding the lead. A short distance to be sure, but he will be walking.

Each time you go out, slightly extend the walking distance to your doorstep on the way back home. The farther away you get, the more likely your cat is to start taking an interest in shrubs, lawns, gates, and a whole new world. He will let you know when he is ready to walk away from your house at the start of a stroll by doing simply that. Until then, you can always carry him as far away as you wish and allow him to walk back. Particularly at this early stage, it is best to measure walks by their length of *time*, not by the distance covered.

The figure-eight harness we recommend allows you to apply a fair amount of pressure if you need to alter direction or slow down. When it comes to getting your cat to go in the direction you have chosen, do not pull the cat that way; use gentle restraint on the lead to *suggest* a course. Keep the lead taut and simply refuse to allow your cat to go the "wrong" way. Never tug or jerk your cat! He will lie down and metamorphosize into a lead weight. You must direct him—for you cannot order him. Don't forget cats are independent and you admire them for this trait. You are walking them to add a new dimension to their lives; they are not dogs, who are walked because . . . well, surely you know!

People who own dogs as well as cats may find that walking the dog and the kitty together is a good idea. Watching the dog happily walking on his leash will set a good example for kitty and may speed up the learning process. Just be sure your dog is one who will set a good example!

Position is not of major concern when walking a cat, but if you prefer your cat to be at a certain distance from you, you can achieve this by gently nudging him into position with your foot once a good disposition for walking has developed. In general, nudging is a slight annoyance to the cat that will help him comply, but don't overdo it and turn your foot into a major threat.

For most excursions, we recommend a four-foot lead. If you plan to visit a park, you may choose a six-foot lead, but under no circumstances go beyond this length for walking. A longer leash allows too much slack and too much temptation for a cat to try to jerk away or to get hung up on something. And never leave your cat tied to anything anywhere! Always be about, alert, and in control of the leash when your cat is wearing it.

If your cat is not used to being outside, practice some noise training while still inside. TV shows with natural sounds from the great outdoors work well, or have a friend in another room create loud noises at unexpected moments by dropping something that will crash or by shouting. Notice how your cat reacts to this; it will enable you to predict his response outside. If your cat hightails it to some safe perch six feet off the floor, wait until he is more accustomed to booms and thuds and reacts less severely before taking him out of doors. Still, since you cannot imagine all the possible upsetting noises that abound in your neighborhood, you must stay on the alert for frightened reactions when out with your cat.

If walks with your cat take place in the city, always pick kitty up before you cross streets. Stop a couple of feet before the curb to let the lead run out, then carry your cat across. Cats do develop some sensitivity toward traffic. But the pace and casual style that are part and parcel of leash walking do not lend themselves readily to allowing your cat to walk across trafficked roads. In a panicky situation, the cat will follow his instincts, not your commands. Cats can quickly revert to what humans consider their worst behavior. Remember that they are not forgetting what you have taught them, but are relying on their instincts. Always respect that knowledge in your cat, but especially when you are outside with him.

8
Toys: For the Life in Your Cat

Toys are the key to a happy, well-behaved cat. Cats hunt, stalk, and pounce naturally—as you know if you have ever watched a real live game of cat-and-mouse. If your cat has no outlet for these natural instincts, he will find something—your curtains, shelves, rugs, furniture—that will turn your home into an imaginary jungle.

If every time your cat plays you need to scold him to get off that or get down from there, you will quickly become a nuisance in his eyes. This will make it much harder to establish and maintain a good relationship in which you are the benevolent boss. Accessible, appropriate toys can help you and your cat avoid mutual frustration and will give you both a lot of pleasure. They also offer several important benefits in cat training.

One of the goals of this book is to keep the playful, kittenish side of your cat's personality intact. Training your cat to be active with toys helps do just that. A nonplaying cat will soon become little more than a pillow that eats.

Positive play with toys will also help you control your cat's behavior. Having his own toys will not only give your cat a way to playact while using many natural instincts, but will provide positive diversion in order to get kitty where *you* want him. And besides, when a cat acts up in a way you consider bad, there is a good chance he is just asking for your attention. Be interested! Show your cat the attention he wants and needs. By offering him acceptable activities in areas you consider within bounds, you give your cat the pleasurable option of good behavior, and you give yourself an excellent tool for curbing bad behavior. In the long run, your cat will not want to do forbidden things because you will have created an outlet for his devilish behavior that both you and your cat can live with and enjoy. You can gain control and maintain the upper hand while your cat plays games by *your* rules.

And, very importantly, playing with toys will provide your cat with the exercise he needs to stay healthy. Just as you need exercise to promote better circulation, firmer muscle tone, and a longer, more active life, so does your cat.

But most of all, your cat will be a fun and worthwhile addition to your home, and he will be happier for it.

Choosing the Right Toys

Finding toys a cat will use and enjoy is a snap. Your home is filled with things of interest. You just need to watch your cat and decide which ones will suit your pet's personality. Find out the specific kinds of things he plays with when on his own and the kinds of smells, shapes, and movements that attract him. Then show him how to get the most fun out of these objects. Your time investment is minimal, and the payoff lasts a lifetime.

Does your cat . . . chew, sniff, or constantly "tread" on a visitor's fur coat or your leather shoes? Is your down parka a favorite nuzzling site? If so, your cat will like things that are made of real animal hide or fur. A rabbit's foot or a stuffed bird with a genuine feather or two is a good place to start. Try leather shoe laces or thongs. Tossed in the air or hung from something solid, they make nifty attack targets.

Does your cat . . . sniff your lips when you are wearing chapstick or lipstick? This activity may signify more than true love, since many cats are tempted by the smell of petroleum-based products—including plastic. The list of plastic toys is endless! Old disposable razors (minus the blades, of course), the cover caps of ballpoint pens, and plastic bottle caps are just a few of the disposable objects already in your home that make wonderful toys.

Does your cat . . . nose his way under the newspaper you are reading? Does he systematically check out any box, bag, briefcase, or open drawer in the house? Then your cat has a highly developed hunting instinct and needs a good hiding place from which to observe his imaginary prey. Keep a good-sized paper bag around for him. What a great place to play jungle, or to hide, ready to pounce at imaginary beasts on an imaginary safari. Double the fun and put one of his favorite toys inside the bag. But remember: never let him play in a plastic bag, which may become tangled and can suffocate him.

Does your cat . . . think he can knit? We all have seen those meltingly adorable pictures of a kitten rolling around with a ball of yarn. And indeed, kittens do like yarn. Keep your knitting safe from inquisitive paws, but let your cat have his own ball of yarn. Wind it tightly, leave a reasonable tail, and roll it across the floor. Be careful not to let your cat play with a single strand of yarn or string on his own. Cats have been known to eat yarn as if it were an endless strand of spaghetti.

Does your cat . . . have a penchant for knocking pencils off your desk? Don't be a Scrooge. Break off the sharp tip and then make your cat a gift of one. If he knows he has a pencil of his own, he just might leave yours alone.

That is really the trick. Cats love their own toys. And just like children, they take pride in ownership because of their sense of territoriality, which we talked about earlier. It's up to you to sense what your cat is after when he gets into your things and to fulfill his desires with something acceptable to you.

Make play safe for your cat, just as you would for a child. Always check for rough edges, parts that could come loose easily and be swallowed—or anything else that might endanger your cat. Stay away from battery-operated objects, as cats handle toys with their paws and their *mouths*.

Toys for Cats

In telling you how to discover the kinds of items your cat will be most interested in as toys, we mentioned such old standbys as paper bags and balls of yarn. But there are many more kinds of toys sure to amuse your cat.

Commercial pet stores, department stores, and even supermarkets carry an inviting supply of toys for your cat. A general rule of thumb for these is "the simpler the better." Anything with a mechanism more complicated than a bell is likely to break down rapidly under the strain of your cat's curiosity. Toys made of stuffed cloth or natural materials tend to last the longest and can best imitate the birds or mice that will pique your cat's curiosity.

If you don't mind their limited longevity, windup toys can be a lot of fun. Of course, you had better be around for a lot of winding. If your cat becomes heavily enamored of a windup toy, you may end up breaking the thing yourself to gain a little bit of relief.

Toys that are scented or stuffed with catnip usually go over big, but do not rely on them exclusively. Save them for special occasions, as a treat. You can leave catnip toys out, but your cat will become accustomed to their scent and tire of them quickly. If you keep them out of his reach, they'll be more effective in keeping him active—and they'll last longer too.

Before you start worrying about the expense of all these toys, keep in mind the vast array of playthings just sitting around your house. And your cat couldn't care less that they will cost you nothing!

Here are a few examples:

- Empty toilet-paper rolls
- Corks
- Empty wrapping paper rolls with a long piece of ribbon or yarn attached (you wave the roll and your cat chases and attacks the ribbon)
- Wadded aluminum foil or paper balls (be careful with the foil—no loose bits for kitty to swallow)
- Plastic twist-ties (the kind you get with plastic garbage bags)
- Plastic disposable razor handles (handles only, please!)
- Unshelled nuts, especially filberts, which look like baby mice
- Empty lipstick containers

- Leftover fabric stuffed with nylons and stitched up
- Old tennis balls

The good ideas for toys are virtually endless, so indulge your creative spirit. Your cat will appreciate the effort.

Getting the Most Out of Toys

Different types of toys will suit your cat's changing moods, but each can serve some definite purpose. Once you have deduced what kind of toys will appeal to your cat, you need to introduce them to each other and keep up the cat's interest level.

Make sure some toys are small and rollable so that when your cat makes contact with them, they move readily. As your cat gains and loses his grip, such toys seem to take on a life of their own, and this will help maintain long-term interest. It is good to start by helping your cat play with these kinds of toys. Show him how to swat the object with a paw by using your own paw or by gently swinging his paw at it. This will quickly demonstrate "cat principles of motion." Try slowly pushing the toy to the edge of a bed or couch and allowing it to hover before letting it tumble to the floor. This creates thrilling suspense, culminating in a cat attack.

For more contemplative times in front of a fireplace or on a warm lap, try a stuffed toy for kitty occasionally to bat at. If the toy is tied to a string, you can have an instant game of chase, or of follow the leader. Try tossing a stringed toy over various pieces of furniture and making it pop up by jerking the string, creating a few terrifying surprise appearances for your astonished cat. With an unstringed toy, even a game of fetch can be taught to your cat. A detailed method for teaching that behavior can be found in Chapter 9.

Make your cat his own toy box. Any small basket or shallow bowl will serve well. Keep the toy box in your favorite playing room, where your cat can easily see and reach it. Let your cat watch you go to the box and rummage through the toys, so he gets to know that this is where all the goodies are. Cats are highly observant and can be unexpectedly imitative—so don't be surprised when your cat starts grabbing his favorite toys in his mouth and hauling them out for play. One cat we know got so accustomed to watching her owner return the toys to her box that she began to put them back herself!

You may not have the time to play with your cat every day, but the more you do, the better your cat will play. Here are some creative ideas. Try blowing children's non-toxic soap bubbles toward your cat. His look of astonishment will be more than worth the small investment. Try making your own paper airplane and fly it around your house for kitty to chase. Tie a light, stringed toy in a breezy doorway. Use elastic string and double the fun. This is like having a windup toy that's continually wound up. Change this one often though, so your cat does not become accustomed to it and ignore it. You should always try to have different toys for your cat. If you simply rotate them weekly, an old cache of toys will always seem new.

You can spark new interest in an old toy by rubbing catnip on it. (If you can find it, fresh catnip is a really special treat.) But be careful not to rely on catnip to maintain your cat's interest; your time and attention should always be the main ingredient in keeping your cat playful. Let your cat know that you are watching him and enjoying the show. Cats are quite vain and love performing. Humor them and they will humor you.

Cats are able to get anywhere they wish in your house. With their natural agility, sense of balance, and extraordinary leaping skills, they can easily devastate your household landscape. Your prized possessions could be up for grabs. Cat grabs! By introducing your cat to toys of *your* choosing, you have introduced the option of good behavior. Your cat will sense that you understand his needs and will respect you for it. Playing with your cat *is* fun and games, but it can also be essential for a good relationship between your cat and your home.

The amount of time you spend playing with your cat will, in the long run, end up being less than the amount of time you would spend yelling and shooing an uncontrollable animal. And it is so much more enjoyable!

9

Can Felix Fetch Like Fido?

Fetching is considered the ultimate proof of a dog's allegiance—physical proof that Fido will literally *work* for his master. Besides playing with fun things, like balls and sticks, a dog will perform chores of convenience, like bringing your slippers or the newspaper right to you.

Cats do not function this way!

Besides going against the grain of a cat's personality, slippers, newspapers, and other dog objects are simply too heavy for a cat to drag about. Moreover, a cat's interest in fetching is based on his instinct to hunt, not on desire to please his master. So, in answer to the question posed by this chapter's title: No, Felix will *not* fetch like Fido, but Felix *will* fetch like a feline. If approached as a game of pure play and unadulterated fun, fetching can become one of many enjoyable activities for you and your cat; and contrary to common wisdom, it can be taught with just a little consistent effort.

In the last chapter, we talked in detail about toys for your

cat. For playing fetch, pick a small toy that your cat is especially fond of. It must be small, lightweight, and throwable—in short, something your cat can pick up and carry in his mouth or easily grab with his paw. Plastic twist-ties, ballpoint pen caps, small pencils, small stuffed toys, plastic disposable razor handles (lop off the part that holds the blade) are just a few of your choices and are easy and inexpensive to obtain. Some cats are particularly fond of shiny objects; others may like the smell of plastic. Your cat will probably make your choice obvious. But do not use a catnip toy to teach or to play fetch because kitty will be more interested in the catnip than in the game.

Athletics should be approached when one is straight and completely sober. You should remember not to rely on bribing your cat with food treats in any phase of training, but especially in fetch training. This means-to-an-end approach is dog philosophy and will be nonproductive in cat training.

Call out your cat's name and show him the object you want fetched. Here is a fine opportunity for a little name reinforcement. Jiggle the toy about, toss it up a few times, and catch it yourself. Get your cat interested!

Is kitty watching? Good.

Now sit down in one of your favorite chairs, a place your cat already associates with your presence. Choose an area with a hard, smooth floor that will allow the toy to glide about freely. Keep the toy active and clearly visible in your hands at all times.

Are your cat's eyes fixed with interest on the toy? The body tensed for action? Okay. Lightly toss the toy so that it lands near your cat. Watch him play with it: batting it around, pouncing on it, struggling to maintain control of it, but all too quickly losing interest in this inert object.

When you notice his interest waning, call your cat while you are *still seated* in your favorite chair. When *you* have your cat's attention, go to the toy. Make sure your cat is watching you. Pick up the toy and return to your chair, always remembering to let your cat see that you have the toy. From your chair, repeat your throwing routine. These sessions should last a good ten minutes and be performed twice a day.

Once your cat starts to respond with keen interest, vary your throw. Sometimes throw the toy up high in the air, sometimes onto a nearby piece of furniture that is "in bounds" for your pet. Try throwing it flat and spinning it across the floor.

You may wish to try different toys—or to use a few toys in a rotating order—to pique your cat's interest, but try to stick with one toy per session. The idea is to maintain a high level of attention from your cat.

Soon your cat will be so entranced that you will be able to throw the toy almost anywhere! Throw it over obstacles like chairs and couches, and your cat will relish the opportunity to show off his natural agility. Or throw it in a particular pattern, repeating three or four different tosses in sequence. Your cat's native intelligence will anticipate the next throw and kitty will consider himself exceptionally clever! As your cat becomes more familiar with this game, he will begin to sense that the action stems *from you*, not from the toy.

The next step is up to your cat, but you must seize the moment when you see it happen. Watch for the first time your cat brings the toy unmistakably toward you. The first retrieval will most likely only bring the toy in your direction, and not all the way to you. Make sure your cat is watching as you pick up the toy and drop it in your lap.

Make sure you are *seated* in your chair with the toy obviously in your lap before you throw it out once more.

Your cat will be eager to play this game and eager to return the toy to the place from which it seems to fly. Soon he may be catching objects in flight with his mouth or paws, particularly if he becomes familiar with a pattern of throws and can go out for a pass at the anticipated spot.

You can help your cat remember the game by playing it often. Not every cat will consistently place the toy right in his owner's lap (cats love to see just how far they can go with almost any form of catlike independence), but he will usually bring it quite near you. In fact, in a couple of weeks, your cat will know and love fetching so well that he will initiate a game by bringing a favorite toy to you—his favorite tosser.

But if your cat drops a pair of slippers in your lap, please let us know . . .

CANEMAKER

10

A Healthy Cat Is
a Well-Behaved Cat

People tend to think of cats as naturally healthy animals who take care of themselves. And in general, they are right. After all, that well-known phrase is "sick as a dog," not "sick as a cat."

A healthy cat is likely to be a well-behaved cat. When you notice significant behavior changes in your cat, it is often caused by physical or mental ailments. This chapter is not a self-help course in caring for a sick animal, but is a guide to help you make distinctions in the causes of your cat's bad behavior. You must get to know your cat well enough to recognize when a negative behavior change means that he needs your help and understanding. A sick cat must not be held accountable for problem behavior.

It is, of course, imperative that you also establish a good working relationship with a nearby veterinarian. A sick cat who needs the attention of a vet will often show external signs of his illness. Be on the lookout for:

- An unsteady walk, a limp, or a persistent change in gait
- Watery or unusual discharge from the eyes and nose
- Unusually waxy or "dirty" ears, often accompanied by persistent scratching in the ear and vigorous head shaking
- Unusual weight loss or gain
- Noticeable change in bowel movements
- Cysts or abscesses under the skin
- Dull, lackluster coat
- Any change in your cat's physical appearance

Like that of his human owner, a cat's health depends on mental as well as physical factors. A cat who is depressed or in an unfamiliar and stressful situation may express his discontent in physical ways. To have a truly healthy cat, you must be aware of both factors and be able to distinguish between them.

One of the first signs of mental distress or physical ailment often is a change in behavior. When a well-trained cat suddenly forgets his litter box (even a freshly cleaned one), this is probably not a sign of vindictiveness, but one of illness. If a well-used scratching pad is abandoned, or if your cat starts spraying everything in sight with urine, discipline may be less appropriate than a trip to the vet. (A trip your cat will take while wearing his harness and lead, naturally! See Chapter 7.)

Watch for the following changes. They look like punishable behavior, but they are just as likely to be signs of a cat who is ailing, either mentally or physically.

- Change in appetite
- Sudden disregard of long-followed house rules
- Uncharacteristic timid or shy behavior
- Constant hiding

- Urinating or spraying away from the litter box (especially if your cat has been neutered)
- Disregard of personal grooming, or excessive grooming
- Crying out when picked up or held
- Any sudden pronounced personality change

How do you decide if these are really symptoms of mental or physical distress? Always call or visit your vet *first*. If the vet gives kitty a clean bill of health, it is up to you to find out what is upsetting your cat—and discover the difference between an untrained and an unhappy cat.

Cats are creatures of habit; once they decide on preferences, they like to stick with them. After years of established behavior you and your cat are comfortable with, your cat may have trouble adapting to changes in your home, life, or environment.

Maybe some noisy construction or street repair work is causing mental havoc for your cat. A new neighborhood pet may be invading your cat's terrain. Perhaps you have recently moved and your cat has not quite made the adjustment. Or maybe your cat has picked up the scent of another animal on you or a frequent visitor. Any new element in your cat's life could be upsetting, and he may let you know by misbehaving.

During any stressful adjustment period, you must show your cat extra attention and regularly assure him of his place in your home. With your support, he will gradually adjust to the unwelcome change. This is only possible, however, if you have *already established trust* in your relationship with your cat. You may need to go back to the basics for a couple of weeks and use the guidelines in Chapters 2, 3, and 4—with the emphasis *off* punishment and *on* reward and play. Almost as if you had a new pet in the house.

If you have inherited a cat from a previous owner, there are lots of things you can do to make his adjustment easier. If possible, stick with his original name and talk with his previous owner to find out what sort of food he likes and when he's accustomed to being fed. Maybe you can bring along his toys and bed. Get a complete history of his health: when he had his last shots, if he has any recurring problems such as skin irritations or runny eyes. What's the most effective way of telling him no? When you get this cat home, show him his litter and scratching pad immediately, then spend as much time as you can with him. Give him two weeks to do as he pleases. You shouldn't let him in areas or on furniture you want to remain off limits, but in the beginning, pick him up from these areas and start a game elsewhere to divert him.

Cats are much more adaptable than their reputations would have it. In a short time your new cat will have forgotten his life was ever any different, and you can begin his training program as you would for a kitten.

Another common cause of behavioral change in your cat is sexual maturation. This usually begins after the cat's first six months. The toms become strangely distanced from you, and the ladies may start to throw themselves against the wall. Literally! Unless you own a purebred and are seriously thinking about breeding, we strongly recommend you have your cat neutered. This is most commonly done between the ages of six and eight months, but consult your vet to find the best time for your particular cat.

Many owners are afraid their cats' lively personalities

will change drastically after they are neutered. In fact, the changes that do occur are welcome ones. In general, you will have a more contented animal, a calmer, more affectionate cat. This is especially true of the toms, who can become nervous and restless as they mature sexually. Neutering results in a cat who is more trainable and happier in his home. It can also alleviate common urinary tract problems such as cystitis. (A typical uncontrolled sprayer is usually unneutered.)

Those of you who still find the idea of neutering cruel should realize that an unneutered cat who cannot fulfill his sexual urges is actually unhappy. And an owner who allows an unneutered cat to roam freely contributes to the already growing problem of homeless cats.

Sometimes, the hardest problem to deal with is an unhappy, depressed cat. When you find it impossible to put your finger on the particular incident or situation that is upsetting your cat, it might just be that he is bored and lonely. Put yourself in your cat's shoes, so to speak, and try to think about what his day is like. Have you been neglecting him? Is he bored with his environment? Is he simply lonely?

New friends, new toys and games, new house areas for discovery have been discussed in previous chapters, and are all useful in getting your cat through periods of mild depression. But what can be done about the loneliness of the "latch-key" cat?

In recent years, a unique program in some convalescent hospitals and senior citizens' homes has brought renewed health and great happiness to many elderly people. There is no secret to the program. Just bring in a few young animals from the local shelter for a visit and wonders occur.

For your cat, you can provide more than a visiting kitten; you can adopt one. This idea, so successful for people, is perfect for lonely cats—or even dogs. You provide instant companionship for a young pet and instant interest for an old one. And it can be a wonderful way to prolong an older cat's life.

When you bring your new cat into your home, always begin by introducing your pets to each other immediately. It is best to do this quickly rather than let the two work themselves into a frenzy over the unfamiliar smells of a new animal. And it is best to have someone there to help you. As you and your friend maintain a firm hold on the two animals, let them slowly check each other out. Let them sniff each other and begin to accept their newly shared territory. At first, you will see hissing, extended claws, lowered ears, and other signs of aggression. These are normal at this early stage in their relationship.

Now separate them. Lead your older pet to a separate room away from the main area of the house. Let the new addition explore the main living areas. Keep your eyes open for potential danger zones. Give the new kitty at least an hour to wander about and become accustomed to any scents (pet or otherwise) that are already in your house. (Sometime during this hour you should also introduce the new cat to the litter box, as described in Chapter 5.)

Once the kitty shows signs of easing into his new environment—being out and about, not hiding; head and ears erect; properly inquisitive about his new home—bring your other pet back into the same room or area. And let them be.

They are sure to resume checking each other out, and there will be a period of stalking, pouncing, and hissing (or growling, for you dog owners). You will see fights that *look* vicious, but are more for show than anything else. Stay around in case any problems crop up that will require your mediation, but try to let your pets work out this early relationship on their own.

This technique should also work if you are bringing a *dog* and a cat together for the first time. But if your new kitten just can't get used to that big, noisy dog and stays crouched behind the sofa for days, you can try this method. Confine the kitten to a room that can be closed off. Don't worry, he will be used to the confinement and will probably enjoy being in this secure environment where he can relax and gain confidence. Let Fido and kitty sniff and get used to each other's scents through the crack at the bottom of the door. Kitty will feel totally protected and so will not mind this, and Fido will become accustomed to the new scent in the house and calm down.

After half a day of this, latch the door so the two animals can *see* and paw at each other, but cannot go in or out of the room. (A shoelace between handle and latch should do the trick.) Now, close the door and let the kitten get a good night's sleep. In the morning go back to step two (seeing and pawing) for half a day. Then let kitty out. He will still be nervous around Fido, but he now knows that nothing bad is going to happen. With the frantic first meetings past, the two pets can begin to work out their new relationship. Even if kitty is still hiding behind the couch and hissing, he has established enough of his scent in the territory and will feel confident enough to make this his home.

Animals have their own ways of communicating and you can bet that these early encounters are all about one topic: territory. Your job is to be on the lookout for overly aggressive behavior that may cause physical harm, but whatever you do, *do not* take it upon yourself to divide your house into separate zones for each animal. This will only keep your pets from ever establishing a livable relationship and will close the door (that's literally close the door!) on compatibility. The benefits of companionship—the very reason you have decided to enlarge your menagerie—will be lost.

When a human baby joins a family in which there are older siblings, the rule of thumb calls for extra attention to be paid to the older brothers and sisters so they don't feel left out and become jealous of the little addition. This is not necessarily the case with cats and kittens. You need to be extra attentive to the more aggressive animal, whether it is the baby or the old-timer. The aggressiveness usually signifies a call for attention and love from the owner. Any cat who doesn't feel secure in his home will become nervous, unhappy, and potentially destructive.

Of course, a new cat may truly be incompatible with another, but this is very rare. Given a proper chance, no cat will forfeit the comforts of home along with a guaranteed dinner hour and will learn, at the very least, to live in relative peace with his adopted sibling. What we have seen, time and time again, are lonely lives enhanced and older, beloved pets returned to earlier, more healthy versions of themselves.

It is important to know how to assist in your cat's grooming. This activity provides a perfect opportunity for reinforcing the trust between you and your cat, trust that is necessary in maintaining a cat who is well behaved and well groomed. In general, cats are meticulous about their personal grooming. But if your usually well-groomed cat becomes lax, your uncoordinated kitten can't seem to get the hang of it, or your long-haired cat can't tackle the job by himself, you may need to step in.

Most cats enjoy being brushed or combed *if* it is done gently. Some shorthairs enjoy a more energetic approach; your cat will let you know. In addition, brushing and combing your cat deters hairballs, the most common of cat maladies. If your cat is having trouble with hairballs you can also help by adding mineral oil, or a commercial product found in pet stores, to his diet.

Cats should have their own brushes and/or combs, which can be purchased at any pet store. Even the best of groomers can come home with burrs and accumulated grime, so every cat owner will need some grooming instruments.

For short-haired cats, all you need for basic care is a fine-toothed metal comb or rubber-bristled brush. Always comb shorthairs in the direction of their fur's natural growth.

For long hairs, use a fine-toothed comb for the head, legs, and belly, and a fairly stiff-bristled brush for the back and sides. Their hair needs to be brushed backward or against the natural growth except at the base of the spine near the tail; they are quite sensitive there. Use an upward brushing motion on their sides as if you were fluffing them up. Brush long hairs daily to avoid matting.

Many cats will groom themselves after a brushing, and you should not discourage this habit. It is not an aesthetic comment on your handiwork; it is simply an instinctive response.

A cat who grooms himself to the point of causing bald spots or skin irritation should be taken to the vet and checked for fleas or other skin problems. If your cat has a sore spot from a wound, or surgical stitches that he won't leave alone, you can make an Elizabethan-style collar out of a paper plate so he cannot get to the spot. Simply cut a hole in the center of the plate so it fits snugly, but not tightly, around the cat's neck. Now make a slit up one side of the plate, put the plate on your cat, and secure the slit.

A more common problem is a cat who won't groom himself. It is not clear why some cats do not learn proper grooming techniques, but it seems likely they were removed from their mothers' influence before she could teach them properly. In many cases you can stimulate these unschooled felines' instinctive grooming response. Rub a small dab of butter between your palms and then slowly drag your smeared hands across your cat's body. He will painstakingly lick off the light coat of butter and may begin to appreciate the benefits of good grooming.

What about baths? This activity is very rarely necessary. You should give your cat a bath only if he has gotten into some sort of dirt that he cannot clean off by himself. Bathing should not be part of a cat's regular routine since it washes away a cat's natural body oils.

To give your cat a bath you will need plenty of towels, cat or baby shampoo, a pitcher, and an assistant. Before you start, assemble everything within easy reach, close the door, and talk comfortingly to your kitty. Remember, cats do not like water. Fill a tub, sink, or basin with about three inches of tepid water. Place a towel or bathmat on the bottom so your cat can get a grip and feel secure. Use the pitcher to get him wet without scaring him. Always keep your cat on all fours—never dunk him into the water. Your cat is likely to exhibit his worst defensive behavior, so make sure you and your assistant always have a firm hold. You may wish to wear rubber gloves at bath time.

Move very slowly, with no sudden jerky movements or sounds, and gently lather the shampoo into the cat's fur. Rinse him thoroughly with water from the pitcher. Make sure you get out all of the shampoo: if too much shampoo is left on his coat and your cat later licks his fur, he can get sick.

Dry him with a towel, rubbing very gently in all directions. Then brush or comb him as previously described. If your cat is not terrified of the noise, you may use a blow dryer at a low setting, making sure the hot air does not get too close to his delicate skin. Always make sure the cat remains in a warm place until fully dry. Try not to pull his skin unnecessarily and talk gently to him in a reassuring manner throughout the procedure.

Your cat will never learn to love bathing, but he should trust you enough to tolerate it. If, however, your cat is absolutely wild when he gets near water, you may need to have this done professionally—but check first to make sure the grooming shop does not use tranquilizers. Medication should never be used without a vet's supervision.

There is another major health concern that is important to cat owners, but it affects people, not cats. Allergies.

Allergic reactions to cats are usually caused by tiny flakes, called dander, that a cat naturally sheds. Like humans, cats may have dry, medium, or oily skin, and they will flake off dander accordingly. A person who has an allergic reaction to one cat may have no problem with another.

What can you do? There is no absolute cure, but here are some partial solutions that may keep everyone's dander down . . . at least, down to acceptable levels.

- Install an air filter in your home.
- Vacuum and dust frequently.
- Feed your cat natural oils (like those found in canned fish products) or commercially prepared oil food sup-

plements. This can help dry skin conditions in some cats.

- Frequently brush your cat, in an area away from those your allergic guest will be in, and follow up with a damp cloth rubdown. (Use an old soft sock like a mitten for a rubdown treat your cat will love.)
- And for you die-hard cat lovers . . . get nonprescription allergy pills for problem guests.

11
Tips, Hints, and a Cat's Intuition

Every cat owner comes to know and love his cat's individual personality, complete with its amusing quirks and idiosyncrasies. But how to find a cat to fit your personality? While there are no absolutes, there are some general characteristics that may help you choose a cat who will be right for you and your lifestyle.

The first and most important rule is to start with a healthy cat. Here are some basics anyone can look for:

- *Eyes* should be clean and clear, with no discharge.
- *Ears* should be clean inside, and the flesh should appear unblemished. Look inside for wax buildup, dirt, or small ear mites.
- *Teeth* should be unbroken, straight, and near white in color. Bad breath may be a sign of a respiratory problem or another disorder.
- *Nose* should be slightly damp to the touch but free of discharge.
- *Coat* should be shiny and full with no bare patches.
- *Gait* should be even and steady.

Kitty should look alert, but do not be put off if he seems initially tentative or shy toward you. Stand behind your prospective cat and give a loud clap to make sure he has no hearing problems. (Some, though not *all*, white cats are deaf, which would, of course, make training much more difficult.) Catch your cat's attention with your finger and make sure he can follow it from side to side. If he can't, it could be the first sign of any number of health disorders and you're better off starting with a healthy cat.

You should always have a new cat examined by a vet and given all the proper vaccinations. Generally, cats gotten from humane societies or animal shelters are healthy because they have been checked for problems before being put up for adoption. This is not always the case with cats who come from private homes.

Male or Female?

The old cliché about female cats being homebodies and toms being roustabouts does have a basis of truth. Unless you plan to breed, we strongly advise that you have your cat neutered, in which case the difference between the sexes becomes minimal. If you do plan to breed, you will find your unaltered female more placid and less aggressively territorial than the unaltered male. An unaltered male will need extra training to inhibit spraying in unacceptable areas, and an unaltered female will need extra attention when she becomes a mother, along with the difficult periods when she is in heat.

Long Hair or Shorthair?

Many owners prefer the luxuriant beauty of a long-haired cat, but if you do choose one, you should be willing to do some grooming *every day*. When a long hair's fur becomes matted from lack of proper grooming, several health problems can crop up.

Long hairs do tend to be more docile than shorthairs. This trait has evolved because long hairs must spend more time grooming. Shorthairs require less grooming and therefore tend to be more active, but it is still a good idea to groom them and it is a wonderful way to develop a trusting relationship.

Purebred or Alley Cat?

Here are some breed generalizations to keep in mind.

Persians and other exotic long hairs are apt to be sweet-natured and docile and prefer a cooler climate.

Siamese and other short-haired Eastern breeds tend to be mentally sharp, devoted (they often choose one special favorite in a family), and active. Their need for warmth makes them sun worshipers. They are also the loudest and most talkative of cats and insist on a say in any household matter they believe concerns them.

American shorthairs and tabbies are playful and need the least amount of care. They are perfect for homes with young children. This last characteristic is also true of British and European shorthairs, who hold claim to the sweetest of dispositions.

"But my Aunt Sadie has the loudest tabby you've ever heard!" we hear you cry. Remember, these are generalities, designed to give you some idea of what you may expect in different cats. As with humans, personalities will vary in any type of cat—but with our training program you will have a large say in just how your cat's personality turns out.

Cat or Kitten?

Most prospective owners almost naturally assume that they will adopt a kitten; they never really bother to think about it. But cat or kitten is a topic worth considering, and here are some of the factors to keep in mind when making a choice.

Kittens are more easily trained than their elders, but older cats *can* be trained. Kittens require a lot more attention and patience in the beginning, so if you decide upon a kitten, you should be ready to shoulder that commitment and responsibility.

You might wish to consider adopting an older cat. An older cat will probably be preconditioned to house living and can quickly adapt to your surroundings. If your cat comes from a humane society, you may discover an especially affectionate animal who is overjoyed at getting a new home. He will never forget the wonderful person who released him from confinement. Also, at this stage in a cat's development, it is easier to determine a cat's particular style (loud or quiet, active or passive, etc.) and to find one who will adapt easily to your needs.

Getting a cat from a previous home means more of a two-way adjustment than when you start out with a kitten. The cat has already acquired many habits, so you will have to accommodate him a little and vice versa. But don't worry—

any cat can be trained with our program. Besides, you'll get used to each other. You'd be surprised at how patient a cat can be with a slow-learning owner.

Indoor or Outdoor Cat?

You must decide whether your cat will live indoors, outdoors, or both. The key to answering this debate lies in your own living situation. In making up your mind, you must weigh the variables of yard space, access, traffic, and neighboring pets. Should you decide that your cat will live strictly indoors, you need not feel guilty. As long as you make sure there are plenty of places and objects in your home that will take care of your cat's needs, kitty will not know the difference and will never miss an outdoors he does not know. An extra benefit is that indoor cats tend to live longer, healthier lives.

Sometimes a move necessitates changing an outdoor cat to an indoor one, and you will need to help him with the adjustment. Every cat is different, and the reaction to such a change can run from immediate acceptance to desperate restlessness. You need to make this cat's life as pleasant and as interesting as possible. Play every game you know and teach your cat a few new ones. Keep a closet door and different rooms open and available for exploration. Try not to leave the cat unattended for more than half a day at a time until he is accustomed to his new surroundings.

Your most important job as an owner is to be patient if your cat reverts to unacceptable behavior, like running up draperies or not using his litter facilities. With proper, loving attention, these bad habits will take care of themselves once your cat gets to know his new environment. If they remain after a week or so, use the remedies described in Chapters 3 and 4. Don't let this behavior become acceptable out of misplaced sympathy for an uprooted cat.

If you live in a neighborhood where your cat can go outside, you need not worry about special training. While hazards do exist outdoors, cats are very self-sufficient and can take care of themselves in almost any situation. But don't raise an outdoor cat simply because you think it's the most natural approach. *First,* consider any danger factors: traffic, environment, other animals, etc. Allowing your cat to go out can be a fine thing, especially for those who want their cat to be calm and easygoing when in the house, since a lot of energy is spent out of doors. But don't forget that the cat who has not *been* outdoors has never established territorial space beyond the walls of your home and can be just as happy indoors.

Cats *do* have that fabled homing instinct that tells them how to return to your house. Still, as a good, easy introduction, carry your cat around your property a few times and let him see and smell the *outside* of all your doors to help familiarize him with them. Remember to have the leash and collar on during these little jaunts, and if he is trained as a walker, by all means take advantage of it. Give your cat about a week to thoroughly absorb some of those outdoor sights, sounds, and smells and to learn just how his home fits into all this nature. Once you feel he is ready, let him out for short periods of time, but only while you are at home and ready to let him back in at his request. Your cat will develop his own "doorbell" to let you know he's out there, but in the beginning, check frequently for his return, and until he feels secure with this new routine, never let him wait to come back in. "Putting the cat out at night" is a common phrase, but don't do it until your cat is fully accustomed to going out regularly and coming back during the day.

Eating Habits

One of the more common problems cat owners must learn to deal with is the difficult nature of a cat's eating habits. Morris may be the most finicky cat, but there are millions of runners-up!

Cats have highly sensitive taste buds, and they may decide to flatly turn down food they have been eating happily for years. Or they may insist on one and only one specific food for a week or two, and then refuse to even look at the stuff again.

You can keep your cat interested in his meals by rotating foods and flavors on an informal schedule. Your cat will let you know his favorites. Some of your cat's finickiness may be your fault—a bit of dry food, one pitiful, plaintive meow, and . . . you give in and your cat gets nothing but his favorite food, no doubt the most expensive can of cat food in the store.

If you want your cat to eat more dry food, simply refuse to give in. Your cat will crunch away long before he starts to weaken from hunger. Dry food is less expensive, easier to keep, perfect for leaving out should you need to make an overnight or weekend trip, good for your cat's teeth, and a necessary part of a balanced diet.

If your cat turns up his nose at dry food, moisten it to help him get used to it. Begin by adding one-half cup of meat broth, drippings, fish juice, or diluted milk to the dry food. (Use milk sparingly, for many cats have trouble digesting dairy products as they get older and may get diarrhea.) Over the next few days, slowly decrease the amount of liquid you add to the food and eventually your cat will be happily crunching away. Don't forget to keep a bowl of fresh, clean water available at all times.

If your cat is ignoring the dry food he regularly eats, hoping for better things from your refrigerator, give him a handful of the same food already in his bowl. He will sniff it, realize he has lost his battle (if not the war), and nibble away.

Of course, there are cats who want to eat *only* dry food and nothing else. It is best for a cat to have a mixed diet, but if your vet gives your cat a clean bill of health and your cat drinks plenty of water, dry food only should not be a problem. Older male cats, however, should not eat just dry food because it can increase the chances of urinary infections, and you should be firm in mixing their diet with wet food. Do not give in to a pathetic meow—if your cat is hungry and the only thing on the menu is what you have served, he *will* eat. You can help break him in by sprinkling the top with his favorite dry food and decreasing this amount as he gets used to the moist variety.

If your cat seems too heavy or too skinny, check with your vet to see if he is ill or if he simply needs an adjustment in his eating habits. Cats need a diet that is high in protein and fat (higher than ours!), which is why table scraps do not make a healthy diet for cats.

If you want your cat to keep regular feeding hours, try this method. Leave no food out after feeding time and stick to an exact schedule. Allow your cat about twenty minutes to eat whatever is in his dish, and then remove it until the next regularly scheduled feeding time. You may divide a proper day's food allotment into however many meals you wish to oversee, but two or three meals are usually best.

This method is especially effective in helping overweight cats slim down. Just remain strong and don't allow a pathetic look from your cat to weaken your resolve. By holding fast to what you know is best for your cat, you can get him to eat regularly where you want, when you want, and what you want.

Traveling

Once your cat is comfortably eating dry cat food, you'll enjoy the added benefit of being able to take brief trips while leaving your cat alone at home. You can leave him a few different kinds of dry food before you go, or you may wish to purchase an automatic food dispenser. Automatic water dispensers are also available and are a real necessity for those of you who have successfully toilet-trained your cat, which naturally makes the toilet off limits as a water trough.

A young, solitary cat should not be left unattended for more than two days, though an older cat may probably be left on his own for three or four days. Of course, it's best to have a friend or neighbor drop in to check on food and water levels and—just as important—to let your cat know he has not been deserted. If you own an especially noisy cat, you may need to board him at a kennel or ask a friend to stay over with him. A lonely and talkative Siamese in a small apartment will let the whole world know all about his woes and miseries.

Don't be surprised if your cat does not jump for joy upon your return. Chances are, you will be ignored for an hour or so, in case you missed noting that kitty has been just fine without you, thank you very much! After this silent approach, your cat is likely to sit at your feet and yell at you for a good ten minutes. All is forgiven.

Another option is to take your cat along on your travels. Whether you plan to go by car, plane, train, ship, or bicycle, your cat *must* go in a cat carrier. Remember to call any travel company in advance to see if it has special guidelines you must follow. Most commercial travel lines will require your animal carrier to fit specific size dimensions, which are generally smaller than the standard pet carrier you may already own. These carriers are usually available to purchase for a small fee. Travel lines are also required by law to limit the number of animals per compartment, so it is a good idea to call far in advance if you want your cat to travel on board with you. For example, airplanes may carry one pet per compartment (that is, one in first class, one in coach, etc.).

If it is a long trip and the cat must go in a luggage compartment (we don't recommend this on trips when *you* must change carriers!), you might consider getting a mild tranquilizer for your cat from your vet. Also, check with your travel company for any particular health requirements your animal may have to comply with, such as shots or health certificates signed by the appropriate authorities. And always have a leash and harness available for the moments when your cat must get in or out of his cat box, even if your cat is not a leash walker.

Your cat is extremely sensitive and astute, intuitive if you will, and will sense a change in your routine that may signify a coming trip. So before any trip, whether or not your cat is joining you, take care that he does not disappear shortly before the departure deadline. Think of him ahead of time and get him collared, crated, or corralled first. And don't assume that he will be his normal calm self—or his normal high-strung self—on a trip. You may even wish to ask your vet for a mild sedative, but *never* use a spare cat pill from a friend. Your cat may not be able to handle the same medication.

If you are traveling by car, take your cat on a few test runs before the real trip. Your cat probably believes that all roads lead to the vet. Show him how wrong he is. A cat can learn to enjoy car travel almost as much as a dog, but don't let him stick his head out of the window. A good rule to remember: anything a cat's head can get through, a cat's body can get through.

Your cat should now be relaxing a bit in the car and be better prepared for the long haul. Make sure you bring along some of his favorite food in case he gets hungry and decides to cry for his dinner. (If you've been smart, your cat will be hungry, since you will have cut off his food at least half a day before the trip. Cats can get carsick, too! Your cat will know whether or not his stomach can handle eating while in transit.) Fresh water, a familiar blanket, an old toy, and a disposable litter box should all be readily available. But if your cat prefers to stay firmly planted in his travel carrier, that's fine, too. That way, at least he can't hide under the gas pedal!

Getting to Know Your Cat

With their superb, at times astonishing, senses of sight, smell, and touch along with an almost extrasensory ability to feel out situations, cats react to everything. Learn what these reactions mean, and you will be on your way to understanding your cat.

When disciplining your cat, always try to see the conflict

from his point of view and to be aware of outside stimuli you may have overlooked but that your cat has noticed instinctively. What may seem like bad behavior to you may simply have been defensive reaction on your cat's part. For example, if you scold your cat for jumping on a forbidden bookshelf when there is a dog barking a blue streak right outside your door, your cat will simply interpret your reaction as cruel. Your effort will be nonproductive.

Most of this book has been about teaching your cat to listen to you, but your cat has plenty to tell *you*—through voice and body movement—if you listen. And it is information worth listening to.

Cats can communicate a surprising number of things with only one word: "Meow." Broadly speaking, there are two kinds of meows. One is an open-mouthed meow and the other is produced with the mouth almost closed. The open-mouthed meow means your cat is interested in communicating needs. This meow will become harsher as the cat's level of agitation or fear rises. Pain or invasion of territory by another animal can also be communicated this way. A less harsh sound is a cat's typical call to his owner: "Feed me," "Let me in/out," "Scratch me." By listening closely, you may eventually learn to distinguish these "command" meows.

A closed-mouth meow or cat-murmuring generally indicates contentment: "Gee, this game is fun!"; "Oh, scratch me there again, right there. Ahhh . . ."; or just "Hello."

While vocally cats may only be able to meow and hiss, they greatly enlarge their vocabulary through expressive face and body movements. These motions are a large part of a cat's natural beauty, but more than that, they are messages of thoughts and feelings. Here are some clues to help you understand this cat code.

Face: Wide-open eyes and sharply poised ears mean your cat is alert and prepared for any unexpected situation. This expression may, for instance, indicate interest and concentration in a game you are playing with him. As he gets angry or concerned, his ears will move back and flatten against his head.

When your cat is at his most contented, his face will have a soft expression and his eyes may even be partly closed. If his interest is piqued, his eyes will open wide in anticipation and will dilate if he feels fear or anger. When calm, a cat will keep his mouth softly closed. Fear and anger will cause him to draw back his lips, slowly revealing his teeth.

Tail: Like his ears, your cat's tail will lie flat during stressful moments. It will also swish back and forth slowly, often indicating an upcoming pounce. When walking, an alert cat will hold his tail high and straight. This is especially true of shorthairs. The tail of a cat waiting for play will often have an upside down "U" shape at its end. When the tail is lying softly behind kitty, you have a most relaxed cat on your hands.

Body and Fur: Since a cat's fur is attached to the outer layer of skin, where the nerve endings are, when the cat is anxious or upset his fur will appear to stand on end like the quills of a porcupine. In dangerous situations, your cat will arch his back and move sideways, which gives him the options of running away, maintaining his distance, or attacking. The sideways stance also lets your cat see an attacker without opening himself to the complete vulnerability of a straight retreat.

When your cat shows signs of tension, it's a perfect time to please him by petting, scratching, or rubbing his "sweet spot" or favorite place to be scratched. Find this favorite point on your cat's body by simple trial and error. It may be under his chin, on his belly, just above the base of his tail, around his mouth, or anywhere at all. You will certainly know when you have found it. Use it actively to help calm down your cat if you have just rescued him from a serious confrontation. Before a game or just before you attempt leash training, give this sweet spot some attention. And when the need to discipline arises, let your cat know after punishment is over that you have his best interests at heart by returning to the sweet spot. When that special purring motor clicks into gear, you know you have done well by your cat and can turn all occasions into happy ones.

12
Cat Fever

So far, everything we've discussed has been geared to adapting your cat to *your* lifestyle—but if you are willing, there are any number of things you can do to enhance your *cat's* lifestyle. He's come this far with you, and, after all, isn't he the best cat in the whole world?! This chapter is for the ultimate cat fancier, or, more accurately, for your cat.

Everyone knows that cats love to jump, climb, perch, and generally observe their world from high places. Think of the natural environments created at modern zoos for large cats like lions and tigers. You may not wish to fill your home with sandstone cliffs and sizable boulders, but you can adapt these ideas and simulate a terrain that will create an optimal environment for your cat—a cat playground. With the space constraints of modern life, you may have to forego a bit of style, but your cat will more than make up for any lack of artful decorating by amazing, entertaining and delighting you with his antics. A cat playground can also be built in a basement or separate room if you have the space.

Creating a cat playground could be just the answer for that former outdoor cat, who when indoors is a little restless. A friend of ours recently moved to a large city with his two cats after living for many years in a house with a small yard, filled with trees and plants and wooden gates and high fences that gave his cats a natural playground where they could live out their wildest fantasies and catch a real mouse or two in the bargain. What would happen when the owner and his cats moved to a small two-room apartment with no outdoor privileges? How would the cats react to a lack of available prey? Would the rest of their lives be spent yearning for an outdoor freedom they could never know again?

Fortunately, this owner followed many of our playing techniques and found that his cats made the adjustment to apartment life with hardly a missed step. Basically, they were very happy cats, affectionate and playful. But they did seem slightly more docile than before, at least to their owner, and he felt guilty. He was convinced that his cats missed the freedom of their old playground, so he devised one he could build in his apartment. His cats loved his ingenious scheme and so did we.

This chapter is thus dedicated to all true "catophiles." It includes both specific projects and general principles of cat home-entertainment. Once you catch on to the basic idea, you should have no trouble—and quite a bit of fun—making your own cat playground. Let your imagination take over, but always remember that the main idea is to give your cat a chance to engage in his most natural activities—perching, climbing, jumping—in a place that you have given the okay to.

Always make sure your cat is able to get up and down safely from whatever you design without having to trespass on off-limits areas. Be very clear about where it is appropriate to jump and where it is not. Your cat cannot distinguish the difference in cost between a finished cabinet and a rough, home-built plywood playground, but he *can* learn which are "yes" areas and which are "no" areas.

If your cat begins to use the whole house as a playground, immediately stop him with the hand clap or "No!" method described in Chapter 3. And don't forget your handy spray bottle. Take your cat to *his* playground, and when he gets comfortable, praise him and start a little game to show him *this* is where we play. Your cat will realize that life is ever so much more pleasant if he plays where he should. If you have done your job of instilling in your cat a firm sense of what is off limits from the very beginning, you should have no trouble.

Introduce your cat to his playground by placing a bit of catnip there. Add favorite toys and an occasional treat or two. Your cat will be naturally inclined to investigate it, and if he likes what he sees and smells there, you will be well on your way.

But what of the playground itself? What should it be like? Well, that's up to you . . . and your cat.

To design a playground that best suits your cat's personality and desires, watch your cat closely when he plays. Just what does he like to do? Have you got a natural burrower? Is he always creeping under the couch, appearing triumphantly at the opposite end? Does he make instant forts out of the newspaper or nestle under bedspreads like a groundhog?

If your cat answers yes to these charges, maybe he would like his very own tunnel—one that's not constantly being tidied up after him. See what you have around the house for this cat. Maybe a long, tunnel-like box (from those new venetian blinds you just bought) is sitting in your garage. Or you can create a tunnel by rolling up and securing a large sheet of cardboard. Make a few in various shapes and sizes, attach them together securely, and you will have a delightful cat tunnel.

You can build a "cat house" for a burrowing kitty, just like you would for a dog. Find a sturdy box, or build one from light plywood, and cut a hole near the bottom for an entryway. If you want to really give your cat a treat, do some interior decorating for him. Put an old piece of carpeting inside the box, use some twine to hang toys inside, or do whatever you think will pamper and entertain your cat. He will be as happy as a child with an unlimited pass at Disneyland.

At first, you may have to teach your cat how to use a homemade toy. Arrange some treats along the tunnel or inside house to entice kitty. Make scratching noises on the structure to coax him in, but don't force him. Wait until he goes in on his own—he will sooner or later. Throw a favorite toy inside while kitty is watching intently. Cut entrances in the sides of the cardboard or wood and give your cat the delight of making a surprise escape. You can make this contraption as attractive and unobtrusive as you desire through placement and decoration, but remember that your cat couldn't care less about aesthetics, just adventure!

Does your cat seek out the highest perch in any room and lounge there as the world's most relaxed King of the Castle, paws languorously draped over a corner, disdainful of the peons below? Sounds like a likely candidate for an indoor mountain ledge or tree house.

Find a wall or at least half a wall that you're willing to

give up to your cat, and mount two or more shelves securely in a lateral step pattern. Like this:

$$\underline{c} \quad \underline{c} \quad \overset{c}{\underline{}} \quad \text{or} \quad \overset{c}{\underline{}} \quad \underline{c} \quad \underline{c} \quad (C = cat!)$$

The planks for this stairway should be at least fifteen inches by eight inches. Be sure that the approach to these perches is not in an off-limits area. Cover the shelves with carpet, and your cat will have a fine outlet for nondestructive scratching. He will love each level, but watch for one of them to become his favorite perch. Try throwing toys on these shelves to initiate some fancy cat-leaping. "Hey! How 'bout a game of catch?"

And for the tree-loving cat who is not permitted outside? If you don't have the room to grow a large indoor tree, why not build one yourself?!

Use a piece of lumber—a two-by-four is fine, about eighteen inches long—to create a horizontal perch. Be sure to brace it well so it will hold your cat's weight, and place it high enough so it's above human height. Attach to this "branch" (or next to it) a heavy rope the thickness of your fist that reaches to the floor. (You may buy a length of rope or you can create the thickness by braiding together smaller ropes.)

With this rope attached to the "branch" and firmly fastened at the bottom as well, so it doesn't swing too much, your cat will have a real climbing and perching adventure always available. And you will have created another fine scratching outlet, too. Should your cat be afraid to start up the rope, you can help by supporting kitty during the first few climbs. Start him in the middle and he will naturally grip for support and begin to hoist himself up. With a tempting treat lying at the top, he will soon climb for pure pleasure. Remember to use the treats for training purposes only, and as an occasional surprise. For rope-shy cats, a carpeted pole also works nicely. Both the carpeted pole and the rope may be rubbed with catnip to heighten interest.

If you're really adventurous, you can even attach your cat's "house" up on the perch! One friend used his perch as a regular feeding area for his cat because it was the only way to control his *dog's* excursions into the cat bowl. The "branch" was expanded into a roomy platform measuring eighteen inches by twelve inches. His cat always let him know when he was hungry by calling out from his perch. In fact, whenever this cat heard a can open, he would race up his rope in great expectation. That's one way to keep kitty out from under you!

If you like these ideas but don't like the thought of a permanent structure stuck in your living room, you can build or buy a movable perch and climbing apparatus. These are built on a sturdy base and may be as simple as a carpeted pole that leads to an upper shelf, or they may be complicated fantasies of fun. They may have tunnels and boxes with cubbyholes, ramps and obstacles with holes cut in them to make endless possibilities for kitty. The store-bought varieties are very expensive, but you can certainly *look* at these wonders and then build your own for much less. Just remember, you're doing this for your cat—so make sure you create something suited to his personality. Watching your cat on a well-used playground will give you hours of pleasure, making it well worth your effort.

Even if you have an outdoor cat who doesn't need an indoor playground, you can still enhance his life by giving him a bit of freedom. Why not build him his own door so he can come in and out as he pleases?!

There are several types of cat doors that can be bought at pet stores. Or you can build a two-way swinging door at home, a door attached to a frame built into your regular door. The door must swing both ways so kitty can get both in and out. And it should have a light spring attached at the hinge on top or a magnet attached at the bottom so it closes automatically and prevents drafts. But make sure it is light enough for kitty to push through. You will also want to attach a bolt lock that allows you to close off this entrance— both to keep kitty in, if need be, and to keep your home secure. Of course, you will initially have to put kitty through the door when he asks to go out, but he will learn—quickly.

Even easier than building a cat door is to give your cat his own doorbell. Use a hanging bell with a clapper or heavy wind chimes. Set this up (within kitty's reach, of course) outside the door you want him to use. Now, when he shows up at the door or window waiting to come in, go outside, show him his "bell," and with his paw, ring it. Then go inside, without him. At first, he'll just stand there, looking confused. Repeat this demonstration one more time and then let him in. Simply repeat the lesson until he makes the connection that sounding the bell will make the door open. Welcome home!

Final Note

It is often said that a dog is man's best friend. What this book has been all about is that a cat can be your best friend too.

The essential difference between owning a dog and owning a cat is that dog ownership requires attention that *cannot* be overlooked. In the most obvious of ways, dogs need you.

Cats need you too! And a relationship of trust and *mutual* dependency can be brought about in the same way it can be for a dog: through attention. Since cats are basically self-reliant (you can even leave food out and trust the cat's natural discretion in a manner impossible with dogs), it is all too easy for owners to leave them on their own after the initial fun of having a kitten wears off. But if you pay little attention to your cat, he will pay little attention to you.

Think about this for a moment. A house pet's activities consist mainly of eating, sleeping, playing, and going to the bathroom. Except for sleeping, a dog requires human supervision throughout his life for these normal functions. A cat does not. With a cat, you must *choose* to have him join in sharing your life.

The real key to successful cat training can be called "the three As of cat training": attention, affection, and alternatives.

Attention is simply giving your cat your time and patience, helping him make his life as pleasant as possible. In return, your cat will give you the attention that makes owning a cat so rewarding.

Affection will make your cat feel important, secure, and needed. Your cat will know that in all the decisions you must make for him, you have his best interest at heart. This is why you will be able to give your cat a pill or pull a burr from his coat. Kitty may not enjoy or understand your action, but he will trust you implicitly.

And, lastly, alternatives. Being the proud and individual animals they are, cats are always slow in admitting they could be wrong. Some of their actions that you find unacceptable they deem absolute necessities. By offering mutually acceptable alternatives, you maintain peace in your household, and, just as importantly, you allow your cat the dignity of making decisions of his own. It is always up to you to give your cat the opportunity to "choose" correctly.

With this book in hand, a bit of patience, a firm resolve, and a lot of love and admiration, you can help your cat become the perfect pet . . . and your best friend.

Good luck!

About the Authors

Elizabeth Kaplan grew up in a house filled with cats and has developed her cat-training method over the years. She has trained dozens of cats, many of which belonged to friends or people who had heard about her from friends and acquaintances. After graduating from the University of Michigan, she moved to New York City, where she now lives with her two cats, Stan and Russell, who are both currently in advanced training.

Michael Kaplan inherited his first cat, a full-grown long hair, eleven years ago. He began successful cat training for friends who adopted her kittens. She is still alive and well and currently residing in New York City with her son and Mr. Kaplan.

John Canemaker was recently honored with a one-man screening of his animated films at the Museum of Modern Art. He lives in New York City with Puss, an orange marmalade mutt, and Kwabena, a hyperactive Abyssinian.

To Cat Experts Everywhere:

We hope *Good Cats* has helped to make your cat the perfect pet. But each cat is different from the next, and if you have a special tip that works for your particular cat, we'd love to hear from you. Send your cat tips to:

Elizabeth and Michael Kaplan
c/o The Putnam Publishing Group
200 Madison Avenue
New York, NY 10016